The Assumption of Mary

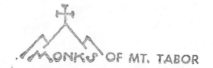

MONKS OF MT. TABOR

THE MARY LIBRARY
General Editor: Eamon R. Carroll, O.Carm.

Mary Immaculate in the Divine Plan
Michael Meilach, O.F.M.

Life in the Spirit and Mary
Christopher O'Donnell, O.Carm.

Understanding the Mother of Jesus
Eamon R. Carroll, O.Carm.

The Assumption of Mary

by

Kilian Healy, O. Carm.

Michael Glazier, Inc.
Wilmington, Delaware

First published in 1982 by Michael Glazier Inc.
1723 Delaware Avenue, Wilmington, Delaware 19806

©1982 by Kilian Healy, O.Carm. All rights reserved.

Library of Congress Catalog Card Number: 82-61438
International Standard Book Number: 0-89453-288-X

Printed in the United States of America

DEDICATION

Rejoice, O people of every nation,
And be filled with jubilation,
For Christ the Lord has risen on high,
Living now no more to die.
Desiring foremost His crown of glory to share
With His Mother ever most fair.
Having been inseparably one with her below,
His first fruits of resurrected victory
On her He wished to bestow.

Having journeyed through life's desert sand
She now beheld God's Promised Land.
When in body and soul He raised her
All the angels of heaven exultantly praised her,
And harmoniously joined the earthly Church
In triumphantly singing,
As Mary's Easter alleluias were heard ringing.
She had come forth like the Sun's first ray
Before the dawning of a new day,
And assumed her place
At her Son's right hand
Where He joyously crowned her
The fairest woman in the land.

Reigning now as Queen forever
She shall desert us never.
For she lives now to intercede
For all her children in their need,
Enkindling for the pilgrim Church
Her ever-burning flame of hope
To dispel the darkness
In which we now grope.
Until that glorious day
When we too will be raised
And join with her in eternally singing God's praise.

Sr. Mary Jane Winkler, O. Carm.

Acknowledgements

To Father Eamon R. Carroll, O. Carm., who not only suggested the subject of this book, but offered many helpful suggestions.

To the Carmelite Nuns of Hudson, Wisconsin, for their hospitality and for typing the manuscript.

Contents

Editorial Note

THE PLACE of the Mother of Jesus in Christian thought and life is receiving revigorated attention in many respects, catechetically, liturgically and ecumenically. Publisher Michael Glazier is bringing out a new series, *The Mary Library,* on the Blessed Virgin in response to the growing interest in her. Very competent authors have been invited to explore important aspects of the mystery of Mary, Mother of Christ, model of the Church. These compact studies bring out the special significance of the Mother of Jesus in God's plan of mercy.

Gospel woman of faith, Mary of Nazareth is the splendid achievement of the saving grace of God; perfect follower of Jesus her Son; and, in the power of his Spirit, sharer still in the triumph of the Risen Christ by her abiding role of intercession in the communion of saints. Many dynamic movements in present-day Christianity have a Marian dimension, for example, charismatic interest in the bond between Mary and the Holy Spirit, and ecumenical concern for Mary's role in Church unity. These and other lively theological themes are being considered in *The Mary Library.*

Eamon R. Carroll, O. Carm.
General Editor of *The Mary Library*

Introduction

In a recent edition of her letters the late Flannery O'Connor, a Catholic and a distinguished American fiction writer, speaks her mind to a friend on the value of dogma: "A dogma can in no way limit a limitless God. The person outside the Church attaches a different meaning to it than the person in. For me a dogma is only a gateway to contemplation, and is an instrument of freedom and not of restriction. It preserves mystery for the human mind. Henry James said the young woman of the future would know nothing of mystery or manners. He had no business to limit it to one sex."[1]

The last dogma defined by the Church is the Assumption of the Blessed Virgin Mary into heavenly glory. Is this dogma a gateway to contemplation? Does it open our minds to a broader vision of the mystery of God and his plan of salvation for all in Christ? Does it give us a deeper insight into the nature, the dignity and the final destiny of the human person? Does it reveal anything about the mystery of the Church?

We believe the truth of the Assumption of Mary, who now sits at the right hand of Christ in heaven sheds light on all these questions. In particular, it answers one of the greatest problems that has ever faced the human race and still puzzles many today. What is the meaning of life? Is

[1]O'Connor, Flannery, *The Habit of Being,* letters edited with an introduction by Sally Fitzgerald, Vintage Books, (1979) 92.

death the end of everything? Mary's Assumption tells us that eternal life with God is the final evolution of every man and woman who dies in the friendship of God. At the end of time all will be taken up and transformed, the body and the soul, the corporeal and the spiritual. For all that God created is sacred and loved. Where Mary is, all the elect will be. Whoever contemplates this mystery learns much about God, Christ, Mary, the Church and oneself.

So important is this mystery that the eminent Carl Jung, psychologist and believer, although not Catholic, could say thirty or more years ago that the declaration of the dogma of the Assumption is the most important religious event since the Reformation. For him it came at a time when the spiritual and psychic heritage of humankind was at stake and in danger of annihilation. He felt that the materialistic view of the world combined with the progress of science and technology endangered the mysterious deeper nature of the spiritual person. The Church and the world need a feminine symbol.[2] Today with the threat of nuclear warfare hanging over our heads, and the widespread disrespect for the right to life in all its stages, we still need the feminine symbol.

God's answer is the Virgin Mary. In following Christ a purely human model is helpful. We need one who walked in the darkness of faith and never despaired, one who obeyed and never deserted, one who loved and was never unfaithful. We need the example of the perfect disciple, and Mary is the first and the most perfect disciple of Christ.

Taken up into heaven after her earthly life the Virgin Mary remains for us the symbol of all that we should be, and of all that we will be, if only we are faithful to Christ.

---

[2]Jung, C.J., *The Collected Works of C.J. Jung,* vol. 11 (1969). *Psychology and Religion: West and East,* 464. Jung made many statements about the proclamation of the Assumption in relation to his views of psychology and religion. Catholics would not agree with all of them, especially his view of the Assumption, in which he seems to wish the Church had gone further and introduced Mary into the Trinity. Cf. Thomas A. O'Meara, O.P., *Mary in Protestant and Catholic Theology,* (1966) 102n.54.

She is the woman in the life of Christ and the woman in the life of all who follow him.

On earth Mary was the mother of Jesus and his wholehearted companion, his comfort and joy. Now in heaven close to Jesus, she watches over us with a mother's care and intercedes for us. She is our life, our sweetness and our hope. She is our shining example. Where she is, we shall be. God knows we need the woman clothed in glory.

It is the purpose of this study to contemplate the Virgin Mary in her heavenly glory. Our reflections will go beyond the mystery of the Assumption in itself to comtemplate the Mother of God in glory in relation to Christ and the Church. For Mary in glory is close to Christ and the people of God. We hope to penetrate more deeply this twofold mystery.

To facilitate our task we divide the study into two parts. In this we follow the model of Chapter eight of the Constitution on the Church of the Second Vatican Council.[3] There as here, Mary is considered first in the mystery of Christ and then in the mystery of the Church.

The first part is actually a commentary on the Apostolic Constitution *Munificentissimus Deus* that defined the dogma of the Assumption.[4] It is here we perceive that the Assumption is not an isolated privilege granted to Mary, but one that is intimately joined with the person and mission of Christ. Her triumphal entrance into glory is part of Christ's victory over sin and death.

[3]Throughout this work we will refer to the *Constitution on the Church* as *Lumen Gentium,* and follow the translation of all the Council documents in *Documents of Vatican II* edited by Walter M. Abbott, S.J. For references *Lumen Gentium* will be abbreviated *LG*.

[4]Throughout the study we will refer to the document of the definition of the Assumption as the Apostolic Constitution, the Bull, and by its Latin title *Munificentissimus Deus*. It is called a Constitution because it legislates for the entire Roman Catholic Church. It is "apostolic" because the Holy Father uses his supreme authority derived from the Apostles. It is called a papal "bull" because it is a solemn pontifical document written on parchment and sealed with the papal seal called *bulla* in Latin, and 'bull' in translation. Cf. *Apostolic Constitution Munificentissimus Deus in AAS,* 42(1950)754-771. English translation used in this study is in *The Catholic Mind,* 49(1951)65-78. We will refer to this as *MD* with pagination from the English translation.

In the first chapter we shall consider the immediate causes and circumstances that led to the definition of the dogma. This will be followed by an explanation of the dogma, pointing out precisely what was and what was not defined. Our final three chapters in this section will consider the multiple reasons in the Constitution that clearly manifest that the Assumption is a truth revealed by God and contained in the deposit of faith that was closed with the death of the last Apostle.

One of the benefits of the definition of the dogma was that it led Catholic thinkers to ponder more deeply the relation of Mary to the Church. So in the second part we go beyond the Constitution and we ponder the Immaculate Virgin in heaven in relation to the mystery of the Church. Our first consideration will be Mary in heaven as the model, image and beginning of the pilgrim Church. This will be followed by her relation to the suffering and heavenly Church. Our final chapter will ponder the texts of the liturgical feast of the Assumption. It is in the liturgy of the feast that we experience God's love for the human family; Mary's inseparable union with Christ her son and savior, and the joy that we are called to experience once our pilgrimage of faith is over. For, taken up to heaven we join Mary in the communion of saints in union with Christ our Lord.

There is no chapter on the Assumption and ecumenism for the reason that throughout the study we have always kept the ecumenical dimension in mind, making a conscientious effort to explain the Catholic position in a way that would be helpful to those who sincerely study it yet differ.

Part One
The Assumption in the Mystery of Christ

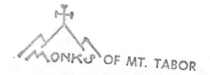

Chapter I
Pope Pius XII and the Assumption

In the bright, mild sunshine that bathed the square of St. Peter's Basilica in Rome on the afternoon of November 1, 1950 His Holiness, Pope Pius XII, defined the dogma of the Assumption of the Blessed Virgin Mary. "The Immaculate Mother of God, the ever-Virgin Mary, having completed the course of her earthly life was assumed body and soul into heavenly glory."[1]

Surrounding the Holy Father on this august occasion were thirty-nine Cardinals and five hundred and seventy-five Archbishops and Bishops. They were joined by an enormous throng of their priests and faithful from all parts of the Catholic world that extended almost to the Tiber river.

But elsewhere the proclamation of the dogma was not received with joy. For, there are many people outside the Roman Catholic Church who believe that Mary, the Mother of Jesus, is in heaven. They see no reason to doubt this, but no reason either to inquire about the nature of her heavenly presence. It is enough to know that she is there.

Therefore, they rejected the dogmatic definition of the Holy Father. For them, as a magisterial declaration, it is unnecessary, unscriptural, inopportune, and even offensive.

[1]*MD,* 77.

This prompts us to ask why did the Holy Father in the middle of the twentieth century define the dogma of the Assumption? Were there any special reasons promoting the definition of a belief that Catholics for centuries had openly professed, and that was not an object of a threatening attack from those outside the Catholic Church? The answer is to be found within the Church as well as outside it. The political, social and religious atmosphere in the middle of the twentieth century influenced greatly the decision of the Pope.

When Pope Pius XII came to the papacy in March 1939, war clouds had already begun to blacken the skies of Europe. Before the year was over, Germany had invaded Poland. World War II had begun. During the next ten years of his pontificate the Pope would lead the Church through one of the most agonizing periods of its history. He would witness the vast physical destruction of Europe, the total defeat of Nazism and Fascism, the critical internal struggle against Communism in his own Italy, the procrustean persecution of the Church in Eastern Europe and the Balkans. He would be overwhelmed with grief by the extermination of four million Christians and six million Jews in crematories and forest grave pits.

But he would witness even more tragedy. Turning his eyes to the Far East he would see China opt for Communism and practically wipe out the Catholic Church that had only recently begun to flourish there. He would witness the invention of the atomic bomb, and worse still learn of the destruction of the large cities of Hiroshima and Nagasaki, rendered apocalyptic infernos within seconds. In those holocausts 200,000 people were destined to die, and countless others suffered bodily burns that scarred them for life. Awe settled over the whole world as the implications of nuclear warfare loomed for the future of the human race. Darkness, suffering paralyzed the cities and all Japan. Gloom settled over the whole world. Each year since then on August sixth the bells of Hiroshima toll to recall man's cruelty to man.

But even after the war ended in 1946, and the titanic task

of rebuilding lives, homes and cities began, Communism continued to harass the Church, especially in Europe. The Cardinal of Hungary, Joseph Mindszenty, was sentenced to life imprisonment by a Communist regime. And in Yugoslavia the Archbishop of Zagreb, Aloysius Stepinac, was condemned on false charges by a similar totalitarian regime to sixteen years in prison. In all of Eastern Europe the Church became the Church of Silence.

But the Pope's interior anguish did not stop here. There were maladies festering inside the Church that needed attention. And on August 12, 1950 His Holiness issued the encyclical letter *Humani Generis* in an attempt to correct certain philosophical and theological opinions in Catholic circles.[2] Directed to all the bishops of the Church, his letter was not a condemnation of any theologians, but the plea of a solicitous shepherd who wished to clear up confusion and restore intellectual serenity in those regions where it was being disturbed. Among other matters, he touched upon the doctrine of evolution, at least in so far as it rejects all that is absolute, certain and unchangeable; the false historicism which is concerned only with events of human life; the rejection of the Church's teaching office; dogmatic relativism; the denial that the world had a beginning or that its creation was a free act of God. These and other subjects touching on ideas considered to be contrary to Catholic belief are enough to indicate that the Holy Father felt the very foundations of the Church were being threatened. This anxiety for the integrity of the Faith so disturbed him that we are not surprised that on occasion he referred to his pontificate as a crown of thorns.

As we review this partial litany of tragedies and anxieties one wonders in what direction would the Holy Father steer the barque of Peter? As the year 1950 drew near, his Holiness saw a golden opportunity to revitalize the Church. Following a centuries old custom going back to the year 1300, he would declare a Holy Year.

World War II was over, people had left their under-

[2]*Humani Generis,* in *AAS,* 42 (1950).

ground shelters, the lights were on again, and a desire for a new and better life was burning brightly in the hearts of many. It was an ideal time to call all sincere people to a year of return from apostasy and sin. So it was that the Pope declared 1950 a Jubilee year. It was to be a year of the Great Return, a year of the Great Pardon, as he said in his Christmas message of 1949. He appealed not only to the faithful but to people of good will everywhere to turn to God again, and to make reparation for the sins committed against the dignity of the human race. His Church accepted the challenge. The heart of the Pontiff was warmed by the enthusiastic throngs from many nations that came to Rome on pilgrimage and by the many more unable to make the journey, some because of political repression, who responded to his call in their native lands.

In this plea for the Great Return the Holy Father was mindful of the part the Blessed Virgin Mary could play. He was keenly aware that for more than a century Mary had had a predominant role in the devotional life of his flock. Like many of his immediate predecessors he had been inspired by the growing number of pilgrims who frequented Lourdes, Fatima and other Marian shrines. Indeed, he himself as Papal Legate had visited Lourdes in 1937 and had witnessed the outpouring of faith among the people. Had he not also responded wholeheartedly to the voices from many parts when asked to consecrate the world to the Immaculate Heart of Mary during the darkest days of World War II? Addressing the world by radio on October 31, 1942 the twenty-fifth anniversary of the appearances of Our Lady of Fatima, he had placed the world in the hands of the Blessed Virgin Mary with the prayer that her love and patronage might hasten the triumph of God's kingdom.[3]

With the Blessed Virgin Mary playing so important a part in his pontificate, it could be expected, then, that he would turn his gaze upon her during the Holy Year of 1950. But this time we find him concerned with the mystery

[3]*AAS,* 34(1942)345-346.

of the Assumption of the Blessed Virgin Mary into heaven. To understand this we must remember that one of the strongest currents in Marian piety to appear in the last half of the nineteenth century and in the first half of the twentieth century was the manifestation of devotion to Mary under the title of her Assumption into heaven.

Ever since the definition of the Immaculate Conception in 1854, a strong Assumptionist movement had begun to swell among the faithful, the pastors and even among some officials of nations. The constant petition that peaked at the time of Pius XII sought the definition of Our Lady's Assumption. Nearly two hundred bishops attending the First Vatican Council had signed a petition, although the Council did not take up the matter. And after World War I the movement became stronger. Finally, all petitions that reached the Holy See between 1849 and 1940 were collected and edited at the Vatican in two big volumes.[4]

The majority of the petitions do not specify the object of the definition. Frequently there is an intermingling of thoughts on the death, resurrection and assumption of Our Lady. Yet, in spite of the lack of precision, the petitions do show a remarkable consensus on faith in Mary's bodily assumption.

On May 1, 1946, Pope Pius XII, following the method used by Pope Pius IX in preparation for the definition of the Immaculate Conception, sent a letter to the bishops asking their thoughts about the Assumption. He asked two questions: "Do you, Venerable Brethren, in your outstanding wisdom and prudence, judge that the bodily Assumption of the Blessed Virgin can be proposed and defined as a dogma of the faith? Do you, with your clergy and people, desire it?"

The answer to both questions was affirmative, and by August 1950 the replies ran as follows: Affirmative, 1169 of 1181 residential bishops. Of the negative answers, only

---

[4]Hentrich, G., S.J. and deMoos, R.G., S.J., *Petitiones de corporea B.V. Mariae in coelum definienda ad Sanctam Sedem delatae* (Typis polyglottis Vaticanis, 1942), 2 vols.

six hesitated on the revealed character of the Assumption; the others wondered whether a definition was opportune. A similar proportion obtained for the titular bishops, abbots, vicars apostolic, and other prelates who had been consulted.[5]

This almost unanimous affirmative response of the bishops was complemented by the devotional life of the people. They expressed their piety in many ways. They were frequenting the churches on August 15 to celebrate the Feast of the Assumption. They were reciting a decade of the Rosary in honor of Mary's Assumption in their private prayer. And under the title of the Assumption Mary had become the patroness of nations, churches, and religious congregations. One recalls, for example, the founding of the Congregation of the Augustinians of the Assumption, known as the Assumptionist Fathers in France in 1850. Scholars of this Congregation like Father Jugie, have done much to enrich our knowledge of the doctrine of the Assumption in the history of the Church. To this Congregation a number of religious communities of Sisters have been affiliated since their origin. Finally, we cannot forget that the Assumption became a favorite theme that inspired more and more artistic paintings.

And so, in this Marian atmosphere, it came as no surprise that toward the end of the Holy Year of 1950 Pope Pius XII—mindful of the human misery caused by the war, of the ever present threat of materialism and the decline of moral life, and of the internal problems that disturbed the Church, turned to Mary, confident of her intercession. As a pledge of the devotion of all the faithful and of his own personal love for her, he thus decided to honor her with a special title. He would declare a dogma of the faith the centuries-old belief of the universal Church, namely that Mary in her whole person was in heavenly glory.

[5]Carroll, Eamon R., O. Carm., "Papal infallibility and the Marian Definitions." *Carmelus,* 26(1979)231.

At the same time he saw in this pronouncement certain inspirational advantages. First, such a declaration afforded an opportunity to give public glory to God, the fountain of all goodness, the giver of all gifts, including the great gift of Mary to the world. Then too, he hoped that it would increase devotion to Mary, so that others would be inspired to follow her in her complete dedication to the will of God. This would, he believed, bring about a great improvement in all segments of social and moral life, and eventually help to bring about the universal and lasting peace that all longed for.

Another benefit of the dogma, he believed, was that calling attention to the bodily Assumption of Mary would remind all men and women that the human body is sacred, that the whole person is holy and destined to live forever. As he so clearly stated, the declaration of the Assumption would make our belief in our own resurrection stronger and render it more effective.[6] He believed that this teaching was most necessary after centuries of materialistic philosophy and a certain existentialist school that taught that all life ceases with death. With all these motives in mind, the Pontiff could write: "We believe that the moment appointed in the plan of divine providence for the solemn proclamation of this outstanding privilege of the Virgin Mary has already arrived."[7]

But was this the opportune moment? What kind of reception did the new dogma receive? We know that the faithful welcomed it. This was to be expected since ninety-six percent of the petitions sent to the Holy See on this question had supported an immediate definition. On the other hand, the reaction among Anglo-Catholics and Protestants was not at all favorable. Especially for those who were ecumenically inclined there was sadness, indignation, resentment and shock. From various regions came different objections. We list some of them: The Church had

[6]*MD*, 77.
[7]*Ibid.*

affirmed a historical event for which there was no historical proof. It had raised a pious opinion to a dogma of the faith. It had used the Assumption as an occasion to assert Papal infallibility. These objections may seem academic to some, but more seriously some complained that the Assumption was not scriptural, it set up Mary as an alternative to Christ as another source of grace, and seemed to open the way to further definitions, for example, Mary the Coredemptrix of grace and even to some form of deification. It was in effect, for many, a disaster, another barrier that widened the breach between Rome and other Christians. One report from England said: "We profoundly regret that the Roman Catholic Church has chosen by this act to increase dogmatic differences in Christendom and has thereby gravely injured the growth of understanding between Christians based on a common possession of the fundamental truths of the Gospel."[8]

Once the dogma was declared and became binding on all Catholics it was incumbent upon theologians and preachers to proclaim the dogma with clarity, and to probe deeply into this mystery to show its place in the divine plan of redemption, its relation to Christ, to the Church, to the final destiny of the human race. At the same time they had to put to rest the misunderstandings that had cropped up among those outside the Church, who, in conscience, could not reconcile the dogma of the Assumption with their concept of revealed Christian religion.

What are our thoughts some thirty years after the definition? Would it have been more opportune to have delayed the definition? Do we have in the Church today a deeper understanding of the mystery in relation to Christ and the

---

[8]London Times, Aug. 18, 1950. cf. also Koster, H.M. "Protestant Reactions to Mary's Assumption" in *Theology Digest,* 5 (1957) 105-108. An account of Lutheran and Calvinist reaction in Europe. "Répercussion du dogme de l'Assomption hors de l'Eglise catholique" in *Document Catholique,* Feb. 25, 1951, col. 235-345. The Orthodox Church might not welcome the definition, but could not oppose a belief that had been held in their Church for over a thousand years. cf. *Das neue Mariendogma im Lichte der Geschichte und im Urteil der Oekumene* (1951), ed. by F. Heiler, 149.

Church? How relevant and real is Mary in glory to Christians today? Are Christians conscious of the part she plays in their lives? Finally, have we cleared up the misunderstandings of our separated brothers and sisters and entered into fruitful dialogue with them? These are questions we shall grapple with, fully aware that we no longer live in the Marian age of Pius XII. On the other hand, if our age is less Marian it is clearly more ecumenical, more open and sympathetic to the problems of others. Having said this, let us begin our study to determine the precise meaning of the definition of the dogma. It is hoped that this will be beneficial not only to Catholics, but to those who are not in full communion with the Catholic Church.

Chapter Two
The Meaning of the Assumption

WHEN POPE PIUS XII DEFINED the mystery of the Assumption of our Lady he offered the Church a precise definition of the dogma, but left many unanswered questions. It is our intention to present here some observations on the meaning of the dogma, and then the unanswered questions.

A. The Meaning of the Dogma

Today when Catholics lift their hearts to pray to Mary in heaven, they are not concerned with the exact definition of the dogma of the Assumption. For them Mary is in heaven, and they invoke her aid. If they have an image of Mary in their minds it could easily be drawn from some work of art. One thinks readily of the beautiful early sixteenth century woodcut of Albrecht Dürer (d.1528) at the Metropolitan Museum of Art in New York. In it we see our Lady in regal dress rising above the tomb around which are gathered the amazed Apostles. Entering heaven, she is being crowned by the Father on the right, Jesus on the left, while the Holy Spirit in the form of a dove and in the company of angels hovers over the joyful coronation.

From this and similar artistic presentations one might easily conclude that Mary died, was buried and rose again in glory. All this may be true and perhaps the majority of the faithful are convinced it is. But, do we have here an exact presentation of the dogma of the Assumption that Pius XII defined in 1950? No, these specifics cannot be derived from the definition itself. The dogma of the Assumption binding the faithful says nothing about the death, burial and resurrection of Mary. These are open questions as we shall see further on. The one thing the Pope did define is that: "having completed the course of her earthly life [Mary] was assumed body and soul into heavenly glory."[1]

Artists, like Dürer, following the piety of their day, and before the definition of the dogma, often adorned their work with scenes taken from legendary accounts. They were more influenced by folklore than theology. Yet, the beautiful creation of the Assumption by Dürer corresponds to faith and reality in that it brings home to us the simple truth that Mary enjoys heavenly glory. It is this truth that motivates and inspires people to venerate her and seek her intercession.

Putting aside the theological exposition leading up to the dogma, what is to be said of the language in which the revealed truth itself is couched? Some have expressed uneasiness with the mode of expression.

They find that it does not correspond with contemporary thought. For some the body and soul duality expressed in the definition reflects ancient Greek and scholastic philosophy that is foreign to semitic, scriptural and contemporary thought and can easily lend itself to an anti-Christian interpretation, as if the body were evil and therefore hostile to the spirit of man. Hence, it seems, as they say, more suitable to hold that the whole person of Mary is assumed into glory, since she is one being. Others following the same pattern of thought would prefer to say that Mary is in heaven in the totality of her person or enfleshed reality, or even that Mary in the fullness of life is in glory. It seems that all these modes of expression are satisfactory and avoid unnecessary speculation on the

[1]*MD*, 77.

nature of her person in glory. On the other hand, must we eliminate the body and soul duality? The Second Vatican Council states that man is one being composed of body and soul.[2] The liturgy of the feast of the Assumption also refers to Mary's body and soul in the opening prayer and preface. Is it not true that in Scripture the body and soul are constituent parts of the human person? In a recent authentic statement the Church reminds us of this when it states: "The Church asserts the continued subsistence after death of a spiritual element which is endowed with consciousness and volition, so that the "human ego" continues in existence though lacking its bodily component. To designate this element the Church uses the word "soul" which is consecrated by its use in Sacred Scripture and tradition. Although the Church is aware that the term has various meanings in Sacred Scripture, she, nonetheless, sees no valid reason for rejecting it. In addition, she is convinced that some linguistic tool is needed for sustaining the faith of Christians."[3]

In any case, it is clear that it is the content of the revealed truth that must be believed and not the mode of expression. Like every declaration of the Church the language of this dogma is the product of the culture of the age, and of the prevailing mentality of the times in which it was written. Formulations may change, but not the content. At the same time one must be very careful in changing the formula of a defined truth lest "the unchanging truth" itself be distorted.

Another expression that has come under scrutiny is the word 'assumed' and consequently the word assumption. An assumption literally means a presupposition, something is assumed. For example, we assume that people tell the truth. Obviously this meaning is foreign to the theological connotation of "being taken up into heaven." It has been suggested that Mary's "journey to heaven" would be more appropriate in English, but even this ex-

---

[2] *The Church in the Modern World,* 14.
[3] Letter of the Sacred Congregation for the Doctrine of the Faith, May 17, 1979. in *The Pope Speaks,* 25 (1980) 127.

pression has its drawback. For some it indicates a spatial change, and not the true transcendence of Mary into glory that is beyond sensible vision. Assumption, then, refers to freedom from the limitations of weakness that affects us in this world, and to a state of new life that transcends our limitations of time and space.

It should be noted here that the Church speaks of the Ascension of Christ and the Assumption of Mary. One reason for the difference is that Christ entered glory by his own divine power, whereas the Virgin redeemed by Christ was privileged to be assumed into heaven not by her own but by divine power.

What shall we say about the expression "heavenly glory" in the definition? Is it well chosen? It seems it was carefully selected to indicate the state, the "condition" of the Virgin Mary after her earthly life to purposely avoid localizing heaven as a place "up there" as distinct from "down here." No mention of a corporeal place is found here. Mary has simply passed from a state of earthly existence to a state of glory. How this took place and what the nature of this new state is like is unknown to us. We have no complete description.[4]

As for titles, Mary is never called mediatrix, coredemptrix in the definition, not even in the body of the Constitution. Rather, she is the Immaculate Mother, the ever Virgin Mary, titles that have already been accepted in the Church.

What then, is defined? Mary in the fullness of her person is glorified. She has reached her final destiny. Her life on earth is over, her association with Jesus that began with the Incarnation, and her cooperation with him, in her subordinate role, has reached a perfect final stage. Now her association with him continues in heaven. Scripture tells us that there will be a new earth and a new heaven. "What we await are new heavens and a new earth where, according to his promise, the justice of God will reside."[5]

[4]Rahner K., *Theological Investigations,* Vol. 1 (1965) 220-222.
[5]2 Pet. 3:13. cf. 2 Cor. 5:2. Quotations throughout from *The New American Bible.*

The dogma of the Assumption tells us that the Virgin Mary is already there. It does not call the Assumption a singular privilege of Mary. This expression was used in relation to the Immaculate Conception, but not the Assumption. Yet, the Constitution of the definition of the Assumption refers to it as a privilege, an outstanding privilege, the crown of Mary's privileges. What is meant by these expressions is variously interpreted by the theologians. Lately, it has been stated that the Assumption is a "singular privilege" because this is the sense implied in the Constitution of the definition.[6] Others do not believe an "exclusive" sense was meant. Saints could be body and soul in heaven. They refer to a common interpretation of a text of St. Matthew (27:52-53) that relates the raising of the dead from their graves at the time of the resurrection of Jesus. This is a bodily resurrection, they claim, and was the common interpretation of the text throughout the first four or five centuries, as well as the firm view of many of the Church's most eminent theologians and exegetes from the Middle Ages to the present time. In the words of Rahner: "The Bull nowhere affirms that Mary's privilege of 'anticipated' resurrection is to be understood as being unique in itself simply, as well as in its cause and title."[7]

It has been suggested even in recent times that the cult of Mary and therefore of her Assumption, has been devotion to a myth, that presents Mary as the ideal woman, the symbol of the feminine, but that with the new age of the liberated woman and a true understanding of sexuality the myth of Mary is dead as far as having any influence on the lives of people. The Assumption of Mary, therefore, as part of the Mary legend will fade away and no longer have meaning for the Christian.[8] However, we beg to protest. For Catholics and many other Christians Mary is not a mere symbol. She is an historical figure and a reality. The Virgin Mary lives, she lives in glory, at the right hand of

[6]Goenaga A.J., S.J. "El misterio de la Asunción y la escatología cristiana" in *Marianum,* 42 (1980) 221.

[7]Rahner K., *Opt. cit.,* 225-226.

[8]Warner Marina, *Alone of All Her Sex* (1976) 338.

her divine Son. For the believer this is a reality, revealed by God and accepted on faith. The glorified living Virgin is not a historical fact that we can verify through eye-witnesses. And there are no historical documents to testify to her being taken up to heaven, nor could there be, for the Assumption is outside the domain of the historian and of natural scientists. Television cameras at the time of Mary's passage from this world would have been useless. We accept the Assumption as a reality, on the testimony of the Lord, as we shall explain later.

Fourteen years after the proclamation of *Munificentissimus Deus* the Fathers of the Second Vatican Council reechoed their affirmation of belief in the Assumption of our Lady with the statement: "the Immaculate Virgin was taken up body and soul into heavenly glory upon the completion of her earthly sojourn. She was exalted by the Lord as Queen of all . . ."[9]

B. Open Questions

Having presented the meaning of the Assumption, we turn now to the unanswered questions, especially those that arise when we consider the last moments of Mary's life on earth. How did she leave this earth? Did she die or was she taken up without tasting the pain of death? The answer to this question and others would surely help us to understand better the true meaning of the Assumption. With this in mind we ask three questions: Did Mary die? If she did, where was she buried? Finally, did her body return to dust and to ashes after death, or was it assumed incorrupt into heaven?

DID MARY DIE?

Some Christians outside the Roman Catholic Church who aspired to the unity of all Christians were dismayed by the definition of the Assumption. Yet, they took some

[9]*LG,* 59.

comfort in the fact that the Holy Father defined the minimum, and left the death of Mary and her resurrection from the dead open questions. Within the Church this decision was also welcomed, because there were different opinions regarding the death of Mary.[10] Certain theologians, a minority, believed that Mary did not die, but was immediately taken up into heaven in her whole person after the course of her earthly life.[11] They appealed to her Immaculate Conception as necessarily demanding her immortality. This has never been a common opinion in the Church. In fact, there is a long traditional conviction that Mary died a natural death. We could pass over this problem since the truth of the Assumption does not depend on the final condition of Mary in this world. However, if we take a brief survey of the tradition concerning Mary's final end, then the dogma itself of the Assumption stands forth more clearly.

So, we ask the question: Did Mary die? What is the tradition that has come down to us? Mary's death, if it took place, would be a historical fact. There could be eye-witnesses, or at least some testimony to the fact in early documents of the Church. However, in the beginning there is only silence. In the first three centuries there is no clear evidence in the writings of the Fathers and other ecclesiastical writers that Mary died. The earliest writers are silent. In the third century Origen (d.253) assumes that she died. He mentions it in passing. Later writers like St. Ephrem (d.373), and St. Augustine (d.430) and some others affirm her death, while the opinions of still others, such as St. Ambrose (d.397), are disputed.[12]

The first writer to refer expressly to Mary's final end is St. Epiphanius about the year 377. He writes: ". . . either the holy Virgin died and was buried, then her falling asleep

---

[10] Jugie Martin, *La Morte é l'Assomption de la Sainte Vierge. Etude historico doctrinale* . . . Città del Vaticano. (1944) 59-69.

[11] Jugie, Roschini, Gallus etc. Cf. Galot J., S.J. "La Mystère de l'Assomption", in Du Manoir, *Maria*, 7 (1963) 191.

[12] Epiphanius, *Panarion*, haer. 78, 23 (GCS) 37, 474. Quoted by Walter Burghardt, S.J. *The Testimony of the Patristic Age Concerning Mary's Death.* Westminster, Md. (1957) 6.

was with honor, her death chaste, her crown that of virginity. Or she was killed, as it is written: 'and your own soul a sword shall pierce,' then her glory is among the martyrs and her holy body amid blessings, she through whom light rose over the world. Or she remained alive, since nothing is impossible with God and He can do whatever He desires, for her end no one knows.'' It is obvious that Epiphanius poses the final destiny of Mary as a problem, and his testimony will have great influence down through the centuries. The three possibilities of Mary's final end that he presents, some believe, may well be the three current beliefs in Palestine at that time.[13]

If the first centuries offer no general consensus among the Fathers and writers concerning the death of Mary, what can be said of other sources?

After the Council of Ephesus in the fifth century, apocryphal literature about the final end of Mary began to flourish in the Church and had its greatest expansion in the sixth century. More than twenty accounts of it are extant in Greek, Syriac, Coptic, Armenian, Arabic, and Latin, not to mention derivations in many vernacular versions. One of these is the Pseudo-Melito document that has been characterized as a quasi-official version in the Latin Church. It is often referred to as the *Transitus Mariae* (Passage of Mary), and we shall mention it later in reference to the tomb of Mary.[14] We do not know the author but it was attributed to Melito, bishop of Sardis of the late second century. Various dates have been given for its origin. Some say it was written about 550. Competent patrologists place it in the fourth century.[15] Father Bagatti, the eminent archeologist, taking into account the Judeao-Christian character of the document places it in the third or even second century.[16] Father Bagatti's view is that

[13]Burghardt, Walter, *Ibid.* 7.

[14]*The Apocryphal New Testament,* Montague Rhodes James, Oxford (1960) 213.

[15]Merino Luis, C.P., "The Tomb of Mary", in *The Bible Today* (1964) 17.

[16]Bagatti B., OFM, Picirillo, M., OFM, Prodomo A. OFM, *New Discoveries at the Tomb of Virgin Mary in Gethsemane,* trans. L. Sciberra, Franciscan Printing Press, Jerusalem (1975) 17.

because it originated in a Judeao-Christian community, this *Transitus Mariae* was looked upon as heretical or schismatic, and therefore Fathers such as St. Epiphanius, St. Cyril and others would be silent about it.

At any rate, this literature that began in the East and spread to the West is filled with legends and miracles, often in bad taste. The writers give free reign to their fantasy, and centuries later artists like Albrecht Dürer would find in these accounts rich material for their creations.

The apocryphal literature has never been accepted in the Church as canonical and actually has long been considered with great suspicion. It was officially rejected by the *Decretum Gelasianum*.[17] Although having no historical value these accounts are a priceless witness to the preoccupation of the faithful of the early Church with the death, resurrection and assumption of Mary. What do they tell us? There is general agreement that Mary died, and that her body did not suffer corruption. In some of the accounts Mary is assumed into heaven while the Apostles are still in Jerusalem, in others the dispersed Apostles are brought together miraculously to her deathbed. In some Mary's body vanishes, in others it is interred. In some it is taken into heaven, in others transported to paradise to await the end of time. In the Greek, Latin and Syriac texts the Assumption follows shortly after her death; in the Coptic texts only after 206 days. There is great diversity, but they agree that she died a natural death and exclude martyrdom and immortality.

We cite the following account from the *Transitus* of Pseudo-Melito: "And as the Lord thus spoke, Mary arose from the pavement and laid herself on her bed, and giving thanks to God she gave up the ghost. But the apostles saw her soul, that it was of such whiteness that no tongue of mortal men can worthily express it, for it excelled all whiteness of snow and of all metal and silver that glisteneth with great brightness of light."[18]

[17]Rush A., CSSR., "Mary in the Apocrypha of the New Testament" in *Mariology*, I, ed. by J. Carol, OFM (1954) 167.

[18]Text cited by Merino *Op.cit.*, 1928, also by Bagatti, *Op.cit.*12. cf. James, *Op.cit.*213 (contains the whole text).

There can be no doubt that the *Transitus Mariae* literature had great influence in the Church, and helped to bring about a conviction that Mary died like other mortals.

But even if we should put aside the *Transitus* literature as historically worthless, and suspend judgment about its theological value as an indication of the belief of the people, there are other testimonies to the death of Mary. We think immediately of the liturgy, especially the Feast of the Dormition (falling asleep) of Mary. Its origin is still the subject of study, but it first appears in the East and spreads to the West. It is certainly a widespread feast in the East by the beginning of the 7th century, and the death of Mary and her passage to the Lord is certainly the object of the feast. Most significant is the pastoral letter of John, Archbishop of Thessalonica, when he introduced the feast into his diocese about 620. He wrote: "Almost all the earth celebrates in festive fashion the annual remembrance of her repose save for a few places, including . . . Thessalonica."[19]

The Dormition of Our Lady was celebrated on August 15 and homilies preached on that occasion during the seventh and eighth centuries have come down to us. Some of those cited by Pope Pius XII in his Constitution of the definition of the Assumption testify to the faith of that time, namely, that Mary truly died.[20] For the sake of brevity we cite only the homily attributed to St. Modestus, Patriarch of Jerusalem (d.634). "She fell asleep, she fell asleep, she fell asleep, she who gave birth to the world's life and resurrection."

It is clear from the context of the homily that Modestus is preoccupied with her death: "Ever anguished by the divine desire with which as Mother of God she yearned for Him, the Blessed Mary quit her holy body with Her eyes upon Him, and into His hands she commended her all blessed, all holy soul. As his Mother all holy, she followed him . . ."[21]

Leaving the East and coming to the West, we notice that

[19]Cited by Burghardt, *Op.cit.*20.
[20]*MD,* 70, 71.
[21]Cited by Burghardt, *Op.cit.* 25.

there are few references concerning the death of Mary apart from the liturgy of the feast of the Dormition that came to the West in the seventh century. One influential writer is St. Gregory of Tours, who in 590 testifies to the death, burial and resurrection of Mary. Under the influence, it seems, of *Transitus Mariae* literature he writes:

"After this, the Apostles scattered through different countries to preach the word of God. Subsequently, blessed Mary finished the course of this life and was summoned from the world, and all the Apostles were gathered together, each from his own area, at her home. On hearing that she was to be taken up from the world, they kept watch with her. All at once her Lord came with angels, took her soul, delivered it to Michael the Archangel, and disappeared. At daybreak, however, the Apostles lifted up the body together with the funeral bed, placed it in a tomb, and kept watch over it, in readiness for the Lord's coming. And again, all at once the Lord stood by them and ordered the holy body taken up and carried on a cloud to paradise. There reunited with the soul, it rejoices with His elect and enjoys eternity's blessings which will never end."[22]

To summarize the conviction of the early Church up to the ninth century concerning the manner of death of Mary, we quote the judgment of Father Walter Burghardt, to whom we are indebted for much of the above survey. He writes: "From the evidence of the patristic age there emerges a widespread conviction of the early Church that our Lady died a natural death. This conviction, especially between the fifth and the eighth centuries, was shared by hierarchy and faithful, preached by theologians, publicly affirmed in the liturgy. There is no comparable conviction to offset it, for in dissent we find only individuals, not a tradition."[23]

POST-PATRISTIC TEACHING

In the course of time all the great scholastic theologians of the thirteen century, following the lead of the liturgy

[22]*Ibid.*, 31, 32.
[23]*Ibid.*, 41.

and earlier tradition, taught that Mary had died. Their opinion had great influence on theologians and preachers of succeeding centuries, so much so, that in 1949, a year before the declaration of the dogma, petitions were sent to the Holy See asking that Mary's death be part of the official definition. This petition was never granted. For there were some theologians, influenced by their understanding of the Immaculate Conception, who held that Mary did not die, but was taken up body and soul into heaven as the course of her earthly life came to an end.[24]

Yet, we cannot help asking whether Pope Pius XII believed privately that Mary truly died. Some say he did, and recall that in the body of the declaration he mentions the death of Mary many times, but always as the teaching of others.[25]

What is certain, however, is that a quarter of a century after the definition Pope Paul VI who spoke frequently on the Assumption in homilies did believe in the death and anticipated resurrection of Mary. In a homily, a year before his death, in a parish church of Castel Gandolfo, August 15, 1977, he stated: "She [Mary] died, in fact, but immediately crossed that abyss which led her to ascend to the fullness of life in the glory of God. Mary is in paradise. There she still preserves and multiplies her contacts with us. With the Lord she becomes the Mother of the Church, the mother of humanity."[26]

To this we can add the more recent opinion of some theologians: "To the faithful it would seem almost shocking to suggest that Mary should have been shielded from the humiliation of death which her own divine son so radically and magnanimously encountered."[27]

And if we are seeking for reasons why from the early centuries to our own time the faithful have believed that

[24]Cf. Everett L., CSSR, "Mary's Death and Bodily Assumption", in *Mariology*, II (1957) 463, 466.
[25]*Ibid.*, 468.
[26]*Osservatore Romano*, Aug. 15, 1977, Eng.ed.
[27]Kenny J.P., S.J. "The Assumption of Mary: Its Relevance for Us Today". in *The Clergy Review*, 631 (1978) 290. Cf. also Doyle, Eric, OFM., "The Blessed Virgin Mary and Dialogue with Evangelicals." in *The Clergy Review*, 64 (1979) 353.

Mary died, we can mention two. First, Mary was subject to the universal law of death, for she was not a goddess, but the human mother of God made flesh. Second, one would expect that she would undergo death in conformity with the humble death of Jesus.

WHERE WAS MARY BURIED?

In the above survey there is no reference in the first centuries of the Church to a tomb of Mary. Yet, it is obvious that if she died, as so many believed, we could expect some reference to a burial place. Nevertheless, there is no mention of a tomb among the early Christian writers. Not until the fifth century, after the Council of Ephesus, do we find mention of her grave. Unfortunately, two burial places are mentioned, one at Jerusalem and the other at Ephesus. Even to this day both places claim to possess the true tomb. However, in the light of recent studies the evidence points overwhelmingly to Jerusalem.[28]

In fact, recent excavations (1972) have contributed strong evidence that Mary died and was buried near the Holy City.[29] The tomb claimed to be Mary's is found in the Valley of Cedron a few yards distant from the Garden of Olives, and not far from the Garden of Gethsemane where Jesus prayed with his disciples. It is located in an underground church, the property of the Greeks and Armenians. The original church built over the tomb and later destroyed dates back to the fifth century.[30]

But what evidence is there that this is the place of Mary's burial? The recent excavations beneath the present church, occasioned by the need of restoration after severe floods, have uncovered an empty tomb alleged to be Mary's. This tomb had been hewn from rock and consisted of two

[28]*Ibid.*, 39 "The evidence for Ephesus is meagre, vague, equivocal. It does not justify a confident affirmation, though it may permit a temperate conjecture, that before 431 a tradition existed which localized the grave of our Lady in Ephesus.

[29]Merino, *Op.cit.*1619.

[30]Bagatti, *Op.cit.*17.

levels. In the upper level there were two rooms, and in the lower, a simple small room where Mary is said to have been interred.[31]

What has surprised the excavators is the fact that the location of this tomb corresponds to the location of the tomb described by Pseudo-Melito in the account we mentioned earlier that goes back to the fourth century, and perhaps even to the third or second century. Pseudo-Melito poses as a disciple of John the Evangelist and proposes to give an accurate version of the death and assumption of Mary. With remarkable precision he designated the place and the tomb of Mary. Here it seems that the writer as an eye-witness describes the tomb before the church was built over it. What he says corresponds to the discoveries made by Father Bagatti and his coworkers.

Pseudo-Melito writes: "Rise, Peter, [the risen Christ is speaking], and take the body of Mary and place it down to the right hand side of the city, to the south, and you will find there a new tomb in which you will place it, and there wait till I come to you." "Those who carried the body [of Mary] came to the place of the tomb, as the Lord had ordered them, and they placed it in the tomb and closed the sepulcher with a stone. There they sat before the gate of the tomb."[32]

The recent excavations seem to confirm the old tradition that the tomb of Mary is in the Valley of Cedron, and seems to add some credibility to the *Transitus Mariae* document of Pseudo-Melito. Father Bagatti believes that the Judaeo-Christians, the first custodians of the tomb, used to celebrate the annual commemoration of Mary at the empty tomb before a shrine had been built there.[33] To this day the Orthodox Greeks celebrate the death of Mary with a procession. It begins at the church of the Dormition, the magnificent German Benedictine church, beside the Cenacle of Jerusalem, where Mary's Dormition

[31]Merino, *Op.cit.*1623.
[32]*Ibid.,* 1628.
[33]Bagatti, *Op.cit.*15.

or "falling asleep" is honored. Accompanied by the singing of funeral hymns and the offering of incense, an antique silver ikon of the Virgin Mary is carried along the processional route that leads to Gethsemane. Even Moslems, known for their veneration of Mary, the Mother of Jesus, take part in the procession. On arrival at the tomb of Mary the ikon is raised up on a platform and venerated. "Today a visitor to the Tomb of Mary can walk down the forty-five steps to the subterranean church. Here to our right, facing east rises a mini chapel over the Tomb of Mary. The chapel has two entrances which are connected inside by a narrow corridor. In this passageway can be seen the raised bench mentioned in the apocrypha, marking the spot where Mary's body rested. This place was covered with two marble slabs and transformed into an altar. The roof, rising a little over seven feet from the floor, has a circular design with a hole in the center. The latter is very practical, considering the great number of lamps burning in the shrine. Inside one of the entrances is a mihrab, a Moslem prayer niche, in the direction of Mecca."[34]

Scholars continue to study the origin of the tomb at Gethsemane but there is no doubt that the tradition that has come down to us helps to confirm the conviction that in the early centuries of the Church there was a common belief that Mary had died and was buried.

WAS THE BODY OF MARY REDUCED TO ASHES?

We come to the final problem relative to Mary's death and burial. What happened to her body after death? Did it corrupt? The Church has never made any pronouncement on this matter, and there is no historical evidence. In the preceding section we mentioned that a few theologians (Roschini, Gallus, etc.) at the time of the definition of the dogma believed Mary did not die, but by reason of her Immaculate Conception was taken body and soul into heaven at the end of her earthly life. For these theologians the

[34]Merino, *Op.cit.* 1632.

question of what happened to her body is already solved. Her body did not return to ashes.

However, as we have seen, the traditional conviction in the Church to which we subscribe is that Mary died a natural death. Hence, the question is: Did her body corrupt in the tomb, or was it taken up to heaven without decomposing?

There are different opinions. Some theologians suggest that Mary's body corrupted in the tomb after death. They hold that corruption is the general law for all human bodies, and there is no reason to exempt the Mother of the Lord. The dogma of the Assumption does not demand incorruption. The resurrection of her body does not require that the material of her body in this world, which changed periodically, was identical with the material of her risen body. The corpse in the grave is not the body in heaven. Mary is in heaven with her risen transformed body. For the identity of her earthly and heavenly body is constituted by the one identical soul of Mary, and not by identical material. She is, therefore, bodily assumed into heaven. Her mortal being has put on immortality.[35]

Other theologians would deny this. For them the body of Mary after death was preserved from corruption. It was taken from the tomb and reunited with her soul. They perceive her resurrection after the manner of Christ's.

[35]Schmaus M. "Aufnahme Marias in den Himmel", in *Lexikon für Theologie and Kirche,* I, 1071, cf. Observations made by Bishop Butler in a discussion following the paper of John Saward, "The Assumption" (Oct. 2, 1976) 8, published by the Ecumenical Society of the Blessed Virgin Mary, London, Eng. The bishop said: ". . . If I study what Pius XII actually defined, I find no reference to the incorruption of our Lady's body as it was known on earth. I find no reference to an alleged empty tomb. I am not talking about all the sort of paraphernalia that the Pope wove around this definition, I am talking about the actual definition to which he requires assent of his fellow Roman Catholics. I am not at all convinced in my mind, and I am speaking now as a theologian not as a bishop, that if we could conduct the right excavations we would not find the skeleton of Our Lady somewhere. It would be difficult to identify it, but theoretically it might be a discoverable thing. What I believe is affirmed is that our Lady enjoys, in virtue of her close union with her Son, that fullness of bliss which we all hope to enjoy after the final resurrection, in a sense you have a case of anticipated eschatology."

Hence, her body was not reduced to ashes. There is a long tradition behind this conviction. In presenting it briefly we omit the apocryphal literature, which favors this position, because of its doubtful character, and concentrate on the organs of tradition acceptable to the Church.[36] Many of these have been cited by the Constitution of the definition.

Time and again the Holy Father points out the evidence of belief as early as the fifth century that speaks of the incorruptible body of Mary. There is no historical evidence to prove this, and the Holy Father depends on the theological tradition that has been handed down. He states that the faithful and their pastors believed her body never returned to dust and ashes. The Gregorian Sacramentary sent by Pope Adrian I (772-795) to Charlemagne (786-814) contains the Feast of the Dormition and speaks of Mary's body not being held down by the bonds of death.

Again, the Gallican Sacramentary of the eighth century speaks of Mary's bodily Assumption as unique among men. Moreover, Byzantine liturgy refers to her body transferred from the tomb. The Holy Father also notes that the great homilists of the Eastern Church in the seventh and eighth centuries, Modestus of Jerusalem (d.634), Germanus of Constantinople (d.c.730), and John Damascene (d.750), express their belief that the virginal body placed in the tomb was assumed into heaven. Theologians like Amadeus of Lausanne, and St. Bonaventure also testify that Mary's body escaped corruption and advance arguments to substantiate their claim. The same can be said for more modern doctors of the Church; for example, Robert Bellarmine, Francis de Sales, Alphonsus Liguori.[37] Finally, the Pope recalls that some Fathers of the First Vatican Council wanted to define the incorruptibility of the body of Mary after death. No such definition was made.

Granted the Holy Father Pius XII cited many authorities

---

[36]Galot, J. *Op.cit.,*168. He points out that the Apocrypha favor incorruptibility of the body, although all do not understand Assumption in the same sense.
[37]*MD,* 72, 75.

in favor of the incorruption of Mary's body, what did he himself hold? Listen to his own words: "She [Mary] by an entirely unique privilege completely overcame sin by her Immaculate Conception, and as a result, she was not subject to the law of remaining in the corruption of the grave, and she did not have to wait until the end of time for the redemption of her body."[38] It is obvious that the Pope following the common tradition teaches that the earthly body placed in the tomb did not corrupt but was taken up and transformed. But he does not define the incorruption of the body.

Here we see a similarity with the bodily resurrection of Christ. The body of our Lord did not corrupt in the tomb but was raised up and transformed in the real event of the resurrection. This was a bodily resurrection from the tomb.[39] So also, in the case of Mary her body did not corrupt. There is, however, this difference. She was redeemed by the grace of Christ. Then, after her death she was lifted up by the power of the Spirit of Jesus and preserved from corruption. She is preeminent among all the redeemed. Her Assumption is a privilege, an anticipation of the glorification that awaits all men and women at the end of time. "She was not subject to the law of remaining in the corruption of the grave."[40] In the last century Henry Cardinal Newman expressed this belief in these eloquent words: "Who can conceive, my brethren, that God should so repay the debt, which he condescended to owe to his Mother, for the elements of his human body, as to allow the flesh and blood from which it was taken to moulder in the grave? Do the sons of men thus deal with their mothers? Do they not nourish and sustain them in their feebleness, and keep them in life while they are able? Or who can conceive that virginal frame, which never sinned,

---

[38]*Ibid.,* 66.

[39]Brown, Raymond, *The Virginal Conception and Bodily Resurrection of Jesus,* (1973) 127. He quotes the mind of Pope Paul VI on the bodily resurrection of Christ, p.125, n.213.

[40]MD, 66.

was to undergo the death of a sinner? Why should she share the curse of Adam, who had no share in his fall? 'Dust thou art, and unto dust thou shalt return', was the sentence upon sin; she then, who was not a sinner, fitly never saw corruption . . . her tomb could not be pointed out, or if it was found it was open.''[41]

What then shall we conclude? There is a strong conviction from as early as the fifth century that Mary's body did not corrupt in the tomb, but was taken up shortly after death and transformed by the power of the spirit in its reunion with the soul. So strong is this conviction that shortly after the definition of the dogma some theologians wrote that the incorruption of her body is certain, that in no way can it be held in doubt.[42] More recently Father Pozo, S.J. declared that he does not believe that anyone could reconcile the existence of the remains of Mary in a grave with the dogma of the Assumption. While he granted the validity of the theory that a risen body does not require that the material of the body in this world be identical with the material of the risen body, this theory cannot be applied to the risen body of Christ or to the assumed body of Mary.[43] It is obvious that the continuity and discontinuity between the earthly and heavenly body is far from settled. We shall return to this when we consider the saints in the heavenly Church.

In bringing this chapter to a close, we offer the following conclusions: First, the dogma of the Assumption declares that the Blessed Virgin Mary in her whole person, that is, in body and soul, enjoys heavenly glory. Nothing is defined about her manner of departure from this world. Yet, the general consensus holds that she died, was buried and rose again. Her resurrection is presupposed or clearly stated by homilists. As for the question of whether her

[41]Newman, Henry Cardinal, *Discourses Addressed to Mixed Congregations,* London (1891) 371-373.

[42]Jugie M., *Année théologique,* (1951) Fasc. II, 12. also Alastruey G. *The Blessed Virgin Mary,* I (1963) trans. by Sr. Mary Janet La Giglia, O.P.

[43]Pozo C., S.J., "El dogma de la Asuncion en la nueva escatologia", in *Estudios Marianos,* 42 (1978) 187-188.

body was reduced to dust and ashes, some theologians to-day feel that this is an open question, since the definition of the Bull does not define it. However, there has been a common tradition in the Church sustained by Pope Pius XII in the Bull of definition that Mary's body did not suffer corruption in the tomb. God in some mysterious way has taken her body and soul into heaven. Finally, the definition makes no reference to the bodily resurrection of others.

Chapter Three
The Assumption is a Revealed Truth

THE CATHOLIC CHURCH proclaims in its liturgy of the Assumption: "All honor to you, Mary. Today you were raised above the choirs of angels to lasting glory with Christ." (Entrance antiphon to Vigil Mass). By what right does the Church profess this faith? One might appeal to the definition of the dogma by the Holy Father that we have just analyzed, but he only declares what the faith of the Church is. He did not create the dogma; he did not receive a new revelation from the Lord. So the question comes to this: What is the proof, or the testimony for the Assumption? On what grounds can we say this is a truth revealed by God?

It would be most convenient if we could go to Scripture to find an account of this heavenly event, just as we go to Scripture to find the account of the death, burial and resurrection of Jesus. But if we do, we look in vain. Scripture is silent about the final destiny of Mary. The last reference it makes of her is that she was present with the Apostles after the resurrection of Jesus as they were united in prayer awaiting the coming of the Holy Spirit.

But, in the present ecumenical age, is an explicit statement in the Scriptures necessary to prove the Assumption of Mary? We are told that no well-informed Protestant today could subscribe to the statement: "The Bible, and nothing but the Bible is the religion of Protestants.'' It seems that Protestants, like Catholics, cannot do without a tradition, and that a Church is necessary to interpret the meaning of the Bible. The four written Gospels were the fruit of a pre-gospel tradition interpreted by the individual evangelists according to their own theological views. Even so, Protestants generally will not accept the mystery of the Assumption as part of the faith necessary for salvation precisely because it is outside the Scriptures.[1]

Scripture, therefore, has a very important part to play for Christians in their approach to the doctrine of the Assumption. This has always been true and the Holy Father in the document of definition not only refers to the use of Scripture by the Doctors of the Church and the theologians in their defense of the doctrine, but he himself states clearly that the reality of the Assumption is based on the Scriptures as its ultimate foundation. This statement is vital for understanding the Church's teaching, and we shall return to explain this position when we present the theological reasons for the Assumption.

But if there is no explicit statement in Scripture proclaiming the Assumption, do we have in apostolic times testimony to this event? After years of serious study Father Jugie, an eminent scholar, makes this decision concerning the evidence of the first five centuries: ''We have not found any absolutely clear and explicit testimony to the glorious Assumption of the Mother of God as understood by Catholic theology of our time.''[2] In other words we do not have a positive oral tradition of Apostolic origin regarding the final end of Mary.[3]

Because there is no scriptural statement or apostolic tradition in the early Church, the Holy Father in his definition of the dogma was not able to appeal to those sources. In fact, he does not even refer to this matter. He looks elsewhere for his proof, as we shall see.

[1] De Satgé, John, *Down to Earth* (1976) 136.
[2] Jugie, M., *La Mort e L'Assomptione de la Sainte Vierge*. Etude historico-doctrinale. Studi e testi, Vatican City (1944) 101.
[3] *Ibid.*, 168, 171, 585-589, 609-612.

However, it would be wrong to conclude that complete silence existed in the early Church concerning the final end of Mary. As a matter of fact there was a whole body of apocryphal literature in the early Church as we mentioned when we considered the death and burial of Mary. We recall that as history it is of little value, but it does have some theological value. Some would say that we should study this literature more carefully, for it may contain even some valuable historical information. Be that as it may, here we look at it from a theological point of view. It is probably the oldest written testimony of Mary's Assumption. It was used by the homilists of the seventh and eighth centuries. However, since it contains many inaccuracies both historical and theological, it is not even alluded to in the papal Bull of the definition. Nevertheless, it bears witness to a widespread belief in the Assumption among Christians from at least the fifth century. Father Bagatti, the highly respected archeologist, would place the apocryphal *Transitus Mariae* document of Pseudo-Melito in the third or even second century. But if it is such an unreliable source both historically and theologically, what value does it have? The apocryphal literature supposes a faith already existing among at least some of the faithful concerning the glorious end of Mary. It is an attempt, often bizarre, to explain her last days, her burial and her bodily Assumption. Faith gave rise to the legends. These in turn influenced the preaching of the homilists.[4]

From the foregoing, it is clear that notwithstanding the relative influence of apocryphal literature, there is no explicit reliable proof in Scripture or early tradition in favor of the Assumption. Does it follow therefore that the Assumption is not a revealed truth? Must we say that it is either a new doctrine, an invention, a conclusion from theological reasoning, or perhaps a dogmatic fact connected with revealed truth to which it is related? None of these conclusions is valid. For there is such a thing as im-

[4]Cf. James, M.J., *The Apocryphal New Testament,* Oxford (1966) 194-224.

plicit revelation, namely one truth can be hidden and contained in others, and only gradually come to our understanding. Just as there are many truths in nature that only gradually come to light, for example, that the earth is round and moves around the sun, so in the realm of God's revelation to man a truth is uncovered rather than discovered. For example, the consubstantiality of the Word of God with the Father is implied in the truth that the Word is God, but it was explicitly stated and proclaimed a dogma only in the fourth century at the Council of Nicaea. It is important to recall that there is one central mystery revealed to us, Jesus Christ, and all other mysteries are contained in him.

When God chose to reveal his plan of salvation he did not speak in words; he sent his Son, Jesus Christ. He revealed a person. Christ is the messenger and the message. Revelation is not only what Christ taught by words, but what he taught by his actions, and by his very presence among us. Often the Apostles would learn by being with Christ without forming clear concepts and judgments. They were open to the mystery of Christ, would learn only gradually and would see him in different ways. For St. Paul he was the Redeemer, for St. John the Word, the truth and the light. It is the totality of all the impressions Christ made that forms the deposit of faith. In this would be included his mother Mary. The Apostles witnessed the unique relationship of Jesus and Mary and her mediation at Cana, her faith, her fidelity to Christ as she stood beneath the Cross, and her association with them as they prayed waiting for the Holy Spirit after his resurrection and ascension. They were in some way aware of her place in his life and mission. The mystery of Mary is contained in the mystery of Christ.

With the death of the last Apostle, the deposit of faith came to a close. This deposit is rich but no detailed inventory of all the truths revealed and referred to was ever made by the Apostles. Some truths more evident than others were quickly formulated and proclaimed in the

Church, but even more would be formulated and proclaimed in the future because of the richness of the mystery of Christ. As time goes by, the understanding of Christ and his mission will become even more perfect in the Church.

To express this in another way, and specifically in relation to our subject, the Assumption is not a core doctrine of the Christian faith, but is implicitly contained in Mary's unique relationship with Jesus her son, with whom she was intimately associated in his mission of redemption. Only after the Church came to a more profound understanding of Jesus and his mission could it consider more explicitly Mary and her role in his work of salvation. From this study and contemplation a better understanding of Mary in God's plan of salvation gradually developed. And so we are not surprised that the Second Vatican Council speaks of a hierarchy of truths in which some are closer to the heart of the faith than others, although all are revealed. The Council states: "When comparing doctrines, they [i.e. Catholics engaged in ecumenical considerations, etc.] should remember that in Catholic teaching there exists an order or "hierarchy of truths" since they vary in their relationship to the foundation of the Christian faith."[5]

Consequently, we readily admit a development in the understanding of the truths revealed by God. We acknowledge that only with time do we come to perceive some truths that are less central than others. Among these truths is the Assumption. Another observation of the Council is helpful here. "There is growth in the understanding of the realities and the words which have been handed down. This happens through the contemplation and study made by believers . . . For as the centuries succeed one another, the Church constantly moves forward toward the fullness of divine truth until the words of God reach their complete fulfillment in her."[6]

We hope that these observations will enable one to understand the argument our Holy Father offered in the

---

[5] *Decree on Ecumenism,* 11.
[6] *Dogmatic Constitution on Divine Revelation,* 8.

document of the definition to demonstrate that the Assumption is a revealed truth. He did not present explicit texts from Scripture or apostolic Tradition from the very beginning of the Church because there were none to offer. He did not appeal to the Apocrypha because of their doubtful and suspect character. How then, did the Holy Father prove that the Assumption is a revealed truth contained in the deposit of faith given to the Apostles?

His approach is very positive and in no way defensive. He first presents his strongest argument for the belief in the Assumption, and then offers other testimonies, that confirm it.

What is his first and principal argument? It is the universal faith of all the Church, that is the unanimous belief of the whole Church, the faithful and their pastors. In this faith they cannot be in error. In his own words: "From the universal agreement of the Church's ordinary teaching authority we have a certain and firm proof demonstrating that the Blessed Virgin Mary's bodily Assumption into heaven . . . is a truth that has been revealed by God and consequently something that must be firmly and faithfully believed by all children of the Church."[7]

But does this prove that the Assumption is a revealed reality, a fact? Could not the Church be in error? No. For in a matter of faith held by all the faithful together with their pastors (moral unanimity is understood), the Church is protected from error. It is infallibly assisted by the Holy Spirit that preserves it in truth. The same Holy Spirit that inspired the Apostles in their preaching directs the Church to the full understanding of what is contained in the deposit of faith. In the words of Yves Congar, O.P.: "What the body of the Church together with its pastors, agreed in holding as of faith is part of revelation, since the Church filled and assisted by the Holy Spirit, cannot be wrong on a matter of faith. This has always been the conviction of the Catholic Church both Eastern and Western."[8]

[7]*MD,* 68.
[8]Congar, Yves, *Tradition and Traditions,* (1966) 203, London and New York, cf. *LG* 12.

In his proof for the Assumption the Holy Father offers us an example of dogmatic tradition which is a far cry from purely historical tradition. The historian would like to work back to the historical documents of the first century that testify to the death, burial and resurrection of Mary. These of course are lacking, but even if they were to exist, and he were to find eye-witnesses of the death and burial of Mary, he would never find any documents of eye-witnesses of the Assumption of Mary. Her Assumption is a fact that has taken place outside the natural order and is not the object of historical tradition or of any human science. Anyone who could believe the dogma of the faith only because he has reasoned to the truth from historical reasons would not have Catholic faith. The person of faith believes because God has revealed his truths and we find them in the deposit of faith that closed with the death of the last Apostle. The glorious Assumption of Mary is one of these truths hidden in the deposit of faith, hidden in the mystery of Christ, that gradually came to the consciousness of the faithful, and once grasped was accepted wholeheartedly.

If it is asked how this common faith developed only gradually in the consciousness of the people in the beginning, it is answered that the pastors first instructed the faithful from the Scriptures about the life of Christ that included reference to the place of Mary. The people understood the close relationship of the mother to Jesus from the moment of the Incarnation until his death on the cross. Gradually they began to believe that the Mother of God who was intimately associated with her son in his mission of salvation, who was sinless and virginal would not be subject to corruption after death. Close to Jesus in life she would be with him after death. Thus enlightened by the Holy Spirit, belief in the Assumption of Mary slowly grew. But let us listen to the explanation of Pius XII. "Christ's faithful, through the teaching and the leadership of their pastors have learned from the sacred books that the Virgin Mary, throughout the course of her earthly pilgrimage, led a life troubled by cares, hardships and sorrows, and that, moreover, what the holy old man Simeon had foretold actually came to pass, that is, that a terribly sharp sword pierced her heart as she stood under the cross of her divine son, our Redeemer. In the same way, it was not difficult for them to affirm that the great Mother of God, like her only begotten Son, had actually passed from this life. But this in no way prevented them from believing and from professing openly that her sacred body had never been subject to the corruption of the tomb, and that the august tabernacle of the Divine Word had never been reduced to dust and ashes.''[9]

That this faith existed among the people can be proven from the many testimonies and traces that have come down through the ages. For example, we have the many churches both in the East and the West that have been dedicated to our Lady under the title of the Assumption. There are also the countless images of our Lady that appeared in churches in many lands that tell the story of her death and Assumption. Then too, cities, dioceses, even countries have placed themselves under the patronage of our Lady of the Assumption. A vast body of literature, especially homilies, began to proclaim the praises of the Lady taken up into heaven, not to mention the liturgical celebrations that have been continuous since the sixth century. In the following chapter we shall present the origin and development of the liturgical feast. But here we would like to focus attention on the images of our Lady, easily underestimated as an expression of faith. Artists for centuries have honored the Assumption in a glorious way, and have expressed the faith of the people in paintings, frescoes, mosaics, carvings, and woodcuts.[10]

---

[9]*MD,* 68.

[10]The Assumption was one of the religious subjects that responded best to an artistic genius. Cf. J. Duhr, S.J. *The Glorious Assumption of the Mother of God.* New York, (1950) Appendix, ''The Evolution of the Iconography of the Assumption'' 94. D. Unger, O.F.M. Cap. *Mary All Glorious,* 40-41. A pamphlet (1956) trans. of *Munificentissimus Deus* with copious notes.

The origin of Assumption art is shrouded in obscurities. Some altar fabrics depicting the Assumption of Mary that were known in the eighth and ninth centuries no longer exist but one work that has survived the ages is an embroidered cloth of the seventh or eighth century preserved in the Cathedral of Sens, France. It depicts our Lady in prayer, soaring above the Apostles. She is attended by two angels who hold a palm of triumph in one hand and with the other seem to be supporting our Lady on her journey heavenward. There is also an ivory of St. Gall of the eighth or ninth century that shows Mary in prayer and accompanied by four angels who gaze up and admire her. The artist carved the following words above it: "The Ascension of the Holy Mary."

But by and large the works that would come later would concentrate either on the Dormition or the Assumption of Mary. In the East the Dormition scene, our Lady on her deathbed, was a common subject for artists, and this form of art passed over to the West. The Dormition appeared in miniatures, ivories, frescoes and mosaics. Highly esteemed is the mosaic of the monastery at Daphni, near Athens. But the most beautiful mosaic in Byzantine style is that of the year 1110 in the Matorana church at Palermo, Sicily. There we see the Virgin Mother lying on her deathbed. St. John lays his head on her breast. St. Peter places his head at her feet. Christ holds up her soul in the form of an infant.

During this same period artists pass from the Dormition to the Assumption scene. One of the great works of art dated about the year 1185 is found over the portal of the Cathedral at Senlis, France. Here is the description given by a recognized scholar whose eloquence and charm are difficult to surpass: "Two scenes on the lintel tell the whole tale. The Virgin succumbs in the midst of the apostles, then, three days after the burial, angels come to lift her body from the tomb. The first of the two bas-reliefs is much mutilated, but the second remains exquisite. The resurrection of the Virgin's body by angels, a scene new in religious iconography, is a masterpiece. The pretty angels, in their clinging tunics, free from the weight of matter, are light as birds. They weigh no more heavily than swallows, whose long wings they wear. And they obey God's commands with an alacrity in which there is even more love than respect. One tenderly raises the Virgin's shoulders, while another lifts her head. An angel unable to come near her leans on the wing of a neighbor to gaze upon her. Another sets a crown upon her head . . . For its time, the bas-relief of Senlis was a miracle in European art.''

''The lintel is dominated by a magnificent scene which fills up the whole tympanum. Mary is shown in heaven, crowned, seated at the right hand of her Son. This is the Coronation of the Virgin in its first version. . . .''[11]

Shortly after this, the Assumption is depicted in legendary scenes in the great French Cathedrals. For example, above the left door of the West facade of the Cathedral of Notre Dame at Paris, the door of the Virgin, we see the work of a sculptor of the 13th century (1220). Influenced by the apocryphal literature he reproduces the legendary story. Mary asleep in the tomb is touched by Christ and awakening from death with a gracious smile, with her hands joined in prayer and adoration is raised up to heaven. In later centuries the artists influenced more by theology than legend would portray Mary entering into heaven in the company of admiring angels.

In subsequent centuries, the Assumption scene is still a popular subject for artists. The Detroit Institute of Art possesses a 15th century Assumption, the work of Andrea del Catagno (d.1457). Mary is enclosed in a mandorla, an almond shaped device, a symbol that she is body and soul in heaven, placed above an open grave, which is filled with flowers. Our Lady gazes upwards. The empty grave, her risen body, her enraptured face tell us the moment of the Assumption has arrived.

[11]Mâle, Emile, *Religious Art. From the Twelfth to the Eighteenth Century.* (1949) 57. Pantheon Books.

However, the masterpiece of the Assumption, in the minds of many, and often reproduced, is the work of the 16th century Venetian painter Titian (1488-1576). In a symphony of color and harmony our Lady lifts herself up to the Father who opens his arms lovingly to welcome her, while the Apostles below raise their arms in awe and ecstasy.

Artists of the calibre of Guido Reni, Paolo Veronese, and Rubens would come to Venice to admire and profit by Titian's Assumption. In his own time Rubens would paint the Assumption a dozen times without repeating himself.

Finally, the most celebrated artist of Mary's Coronation in heaven is Fra Angelico. He has given us three different presentations. Two are in the Uffizi Gallery of Florence, the other in the Louvre at Paris.

There can be no doubt that famous works of art as well as less representative ones have influenced veneration of our Lady of the Assumption. Some would say that she has been so exalted in the West that she has been placed out of reach of the ordinary Christian as a model of virtue. She has been enthroned, they say, as a goddess. She is only a myth, unreal. A true understanding of Catholic faith would deny this. Exalted she is, but goddess she is not. She is one of us, redeemed and perfectly human. In heaven she belongs to the communion of saints, although the most perfect member. Moreover, she is exalted as a woman who takes her place by the side of Christ. She modifies any danger of extreme masculinity in the Church. She is the one human being in whom the Holy Spirit has worked with the most complete success. And often it is the male in the Church who acknowledges the superior perfection of Mary, and honors her with great filial veneration. The artists of the Assumption bear witness to this statement, as well as to the faith in the minds and hearts of the faithful.

Serious attention then should be given to the artistic representations of the Assumption. Often they have their faults and need to be interpreted, but they have been a marvelous educational aid for the people. They not only express vividly the faith in the hearts of the faithful, but also strengthen it. But sacred images are only one of the many testimonies of the centuries of faith. In the following chapters we will present others beginning with the Liturgy that under the guidance of the magisterium developed down through the centuries.

But before we do let us recall once again that the strongest proof for the Assumption according to *Munificentissimus Deus* is the unanimous faith of the people and their pastors. This remarkable accord of the Catholic bishops and faithful enlightened by the Holy Spirit existed in the Church for centuries. In a matter of so great importance the Church cannot make a mistake or be deceived for the Lord himself promised to be with the Church until the end of time. Pope Pius XII, therefore, did not receive or claim to receive a new revelation from above, nor did he invent a new doctrine of the Church. He simply declared in his definition what the faithful and the bishops had already believed. In a word, he was dependent on the lived faith of the people. To quote a respected theologian: "It would be more true to say the Pope defined the Assumption because Catholics believed in it, than to say Catholics believed in the Assumption because the Pope defined it."[12] The definition, therefore, does not add anything to the truth of the Assumption, rather it offers to the faithful a guarantee that their lived faith is revealed by God.

[12]Leeming, Bernard, "Pius XII and the Mother of God", *The Tablet,* London, (Oct. 18, 1958) 325.

Chapter Four
The Liturgy as Testimony of the Assumption

THE LITURGY IS ONE of the more forceful arguments presented by *Munificentissimus Deus* to show the universal belief of the faithful in the Assumption of our Lady. For liturgy is an outpouring of faith, an expression of what is in the consciousness and heart of the people. So we look to the liturgy of the Assumption to learn what the people believe. The value of this argument is expressed by Pope Pius XII in these words: "The sacred liturgy because it is the profession, subject to the supreme teaching authority within the Church, of heavenly truths, can supply proofs and testimonies of no small value for deciding any individual point of Christian doctrine."[1]

So we ask what does the liturgy tell us about the faith of the people in the bodily assumption of Mary? Our answer will be given in three parts. First, we shall present a brief description of the argument proposed in the Bull of the definition. We will follow this with an analysis of the argument. We conclude with a brief history of the origin and development of the feast of the Assumption, that will explain the liturgical silence of the feast in the early centuries.

The argument from the liturgy in the papal document

[1]*MD,* 69.

makes no reference to the origin and development of the feast of the Assumption. Rather it presents the liturgical books of the eighth century that clearly teach the meaning of the feast. These are: the Gregorian Sacramentary of Pope Adrian I, the Gallican Sacramentary influenced by Rome, and the Byzantine liturgy of the same period. To these are added the names of the popes who in the eighth and ninth centuries enriched the liturgical celebrations of the feast. The evidence is strengthened by quoting the homilists of that time, especially a classical text from St. John Damascene. The Pope calls attention to the testimony of the homilists because they explain to the people the faith that already exists in the Church, a faith that springs from tradition and that is prior to the liturgy.

If we take a closer look at this argument, and especially at the liturgical books and homilies, what do they teach about the bodily assumption of Mary? The liturgy professes faith in this mystery. It declares that Mary died, rose again with an incorrupted body and is now in heaven. In evidence the Holy Father presents the prayer "Veneranda" that is found in the Sacramentary Adrian I sent to Charlemagne. The prayer states: "Venerable to us, O Lord, is the festivity of this day on which the holy Mother of God suffered temporal death, but still could not be kept down by the bonds of death, who has begotten Thy Son our Lord incarnate from herself."[2] This prayer has been understood in the Church to refer to her bodily assumption as well as to her death and incorruption. For, the phrase "not to be kept down by death" means to be taken up. A similar phrase is used in the Scripture for the resurrection of Jesus.[3]

A passage of the Byzantine liturgy quoted in the Bull of the definition is even more explicit in reference to the Assumption. "God the King of the universe, has granted three favors that surpass nature. As he kept thee a virgin in childbirth, thus he has kept thy body incorrupt in the tomb and has glorified it by his divine act of transferring it from

[2]*Ibid.*
[3]Acts, 2:24.

the tomb.''[4] Mary's body is not only incorrupt it is a living glorified body. The central object of the feast is the glorification of Mary.

The clear meaning of the feast is especially brought out in the homilies, part of the liturgy. The Holy Father offers the testimony of three homilists. St. John Damascene, (d.749) doctor of the Church, St. Germanus of Constantinople, (d.733) also of the eighth century, and Modestus bishop of Jerusalem (d.634). The latter died in the seventh century, and there is an opinion that the words attributed to him belong to a later period, so that some writers speak of the Pseudo-Modestus homily. One thing these three homilists have in common is that all teach that Mary died, that her body remained incorrupt, that she rose from the dead and is body and soul in heaven. St. John Damascene is the most important of these three fathers, and we have three of his known homilies for the feast of August 15. The second and third are very impressive. It is the second that is quoted at length in the Bull of definition. We shall add a passage from the third. ''Today, the living city of God was transported from the earthly Jerusalem into the heavenly Jerusalem. She who gave birth to the Firstborn of every creature, the only Begotten of the Father and her only Son, herself was given dwelling in the church of the first born. The animated and rational ark was transported to the abode of her Son . . . Is it true that the source of life, that the Mother of my Lord, died? Yes, because it was necessary that that which was of earth return to the earth, and be thus transported from earth to heaven, after having received immortal life . . . It was necessary that the incorruptible and immaculate flesh [of the Virgin] pass like gold through the crucible of death, to lay aside the opaque earthly mass of mortality and rise from the grave all radiant with the brightness of incorruptibility.''[5]

The homilists quoted by the document of the definition

[4]*MD,* 69. Menaei totius anni.

[5]Ecomium in dormitionem Dei Genitricis semperque Virginis Mariae, homily 3 in *PG,* 96, Col. 728.

all offer theological reasons to show that it is fitting that Mary should be body and soul in glory. They used the apocryphal legends of the time, but in their explanations of the faith were guided not by legends but by the fact that the Assumption is a most fitting consequence of Mary's virginity, divine motherhood and holiness.

Until 1955 it was taken for granted that the first homily known to us was that of Modestus of Jerusalem. But five years after promulgation of the dogma of the Assumption a most important homily of the sixth century was discovered.[6] It was preached by Theoteknos, bishop of Livias in Palestine, on the Assumption (analepsis, passing over). His teaching is very clear. Mary, body and soul, is taken into heaven. He was influenced by the apocrypha, but reports them soberly, and his arguments do not depend on the legends, but rather on texts from both the Old and the New Testament. For him Mary is the second Eve, who has come to undo the disobedience of the first Eve. Finding in the Scriptures a unique relation between Jesus and Mary he explains that even in death the mother cannot be separated from her son, and he has taken her with him into heaven. He exclaims: "It was fitting that her all holy body, her God-bearing body, this body which received God, a body made God-like, incorruptible, glowing with divine light and full of glory, was carried by the Apostles, in the company of the angels, interred for a short time in the earth and then taken up to heaven in glory with her soul loved by God."[7]

On four occasions Theoteknos teaches explicitly the bodily Assumption of Mary.[8] He finds it to be a complement of the glorification of Christ, and a manifestation of his power. The theology of Theoteknos is solid and complete, and it is not founded on the legends, but on Scripture and sound reasoning.

[6]Panegyrique de Théoteknos de Livia pour l'Assomption de la Sainte Mére de Dieu in A. Wenger, AA., *L' Assomption de la T. S. Vierge dans la tradition byzantine du VIe au Xe siécle,* Paris (1955) 272.

[7]*Ibid.* 276, cf. J. Galot, *Op.cit.*

[8]*Ibid.* Encomium, nos. 9, 10, 1536.

The liturgical books and homilies cited in the Bull of definition offer a convincing proof that the Church believed in the seventh and eighth centuries that Mary's body and soul had been taken into heaven. The added testimony of Theoteknos indicates clearly that already in the sixth century the faithful in Palestine professed belief in the Assumption.

In other words the liturgy of that early period shows that the faith of the Church in the mystery of the Assumption had already come to maturity, for the institution of a feast signifies the calm possession of faith, not its beginning.

History of the Feast

But the question arises: Where is the liturgical evidence in the first centuries of the Church? What happened before the middle of the sixth century? There is only liturgical silence, as far as we know, but it could not be otherwise. Silence does not prove the absence of revelation in regard to the Assumption. It only proves, as we explained in the preceding chapter, that the Church only gradually came to an explicit profession of faith. There were other truths more fundamental and central that first had to be celebrated liturgically. The first liturgical feast, the Lord's Day, Sunday, commemorated the Resurrection. Then annual feasts of Easter, Pentecost, Ascension and Christmas followed gradually in the first few centuries. In the Roman rite the feast of Christmas, December 25, spread from Rome throughout the Western Church from the fourth century. Gradually the Church became more conscious of Mary's place in the life of Christ. This came about after the Council of Ephesus in 431 defined that Mary was Mother of God, Theotokos. From then on we see a flowering of Marian feasts, and these are all intimately related to the life of Christ. These feasts came gradually, and their origin is still uncertain, and this is especially true of the Assumption. Still, our curiosity is aroused and we ask: How did the feast of the Assumption begin, and where?

The East

One thing is certain. The feast comes from the East. One plausible and rather common explanation is that the original feast to honor Mary was a "memorial of Mary" that honored her divine motherhood. This gradually evolved into the feast of the Dormition (falling asleep, meaning death and in Greek Koimesis). This feast finally came to maturity in the feast of the Assumption.[9] There is today no clear evidence that this evolution actually took place. However, there is good reason to believe that the primitive Marian feast began with the Christmas season and honored Mary's motherhood. For, in celebrating the birth of Christ one could hardly avoid reflecting on the virginal maternity of Mary. Thus, it seems that the oldest feast in honor of the Mother of God grew out of the Christmas feast.

Evidence for this is that already in the year 428 Saint Proclus, future bishop of Constantinople, preached a homily there in the presence of Nestorius during the Christmas season and on a feast of Mary. Severus of Antioch (d.538) is witness that in his own city there was a Marian feast between Epiphany and Lent. To honor Mary's divine motherhood with a feast seemed to be a common winter practice. In fact, December 26 was set aside in the Byzantine rite as a Memorial of Mary, and remains there to this day. But we know that a Day of Mary was celebrated in some places, for example in Jerusalem, on August 15.[10] Did this feast evolve from the Winter feast in honor of the Mother of God? Some believe that it did evolve from a general feast in honor of Mary, but not all would agree.[11] How then did it originate? It is possible that the Dormition feast of August 15, as it came to be known, took its name from a liturgy celebrated at the tomb of Gethsemane, where Mary was laid to rest. This tomb was

[9]Jugie, *Op.cit.* 174ff.
[10]Duhr, J., *Op.cit.,* 20.
[11]Crehan, J., S.J., "Assumption and Jerusalem Liturgy", in *Theological Studies,* 30 (1969) 321.

first in the hands of Christians of Hebrew origin, it seems, until the end of the fourth century when it passed to Christians of gentile origin. (Recall what was said about the Tomb of Mary in Chapter Two.)

Whatever the origin of the feast of the Dormition, we do know that it was celebrated in the sixth century in the East. Theodosius, monophysite bishop of Alexandria, preached a homily during the year of his death (d.566) for the feast of the Assumption, celebrated in the Coptic rite on August 9. About the same time Théoteknos, bishop of Livias in Palestine, delivered the homily mentioned above on the Assumption on August 15.[12] In the course of time this feast was celebrated in many places in the East and came to be known as the Dormition feast. This was the feast approved for the whole Byzantine Empire by the Emperor Maurice (582-602) and celebrated on August 15.[13]

In the following centuries the East continued to celebrate the August feast of the Assumption and even today it is the most solemn Marian feast in the Byzantine rite.

What is the object of the feast? Many opinions have been broached. Some have said it honored only the entrance of Mary's soul into paradise. But Théoteknos proclaims the bodily assumption of Mary as the object of the feast, and homilists of the succeeding centuries make the same profession of faith, as can be seen from the writings of St. John Damascene, who sees her glorification as the consequence of her virginal motherhood.

The West

Turning to the West, we find that Marian liturgy developed more slowly. It seems that our Lady was first honored in Western liturgy during the Advent and Christmas season. In the fifth century at Ravenna and

[12]Galot, J., *Op.cit.,* 176ff.
[13]Callistos, Nicephorus, *Historia Eccl.* XXII, 28 in *PG,* 147, 292.

Milan there was a Marian feast on the last Sunday of Advent.[14] Certainly at Rome in the sixth century Mary is honored with a feast "Memorial of Mary" on January 1. Her divine and virginal motherhood is the object of this feast. In the same century a Marian feast of the same nature is celebrated in all the churches of the West but on different days.[15]

For some time this was the only Marian feast in the Western liturgy, so it seems, until about 650 when the feast of the Dormition of Mary was brought from the East. It was not known in the Roman liturgy until after the death of Pope Gregory the Great (d.604). Perhaps it was Pope Theodore I (642-649), a former member of the Jerusalem clergy, who introduced the feast into the Roman liturgy. An early witness is the Gospel lectionary of Wurzburg (c.650) in which the feast of August 15 is found to be "Natale Sanctae Mariae" (birthday in heaven of St. Mary).[16] However, during the pontificate of Pope Sergius I (687-702), a Syrian by birth, the Roman liturgy was enriched with processions for four Marian feasts, the Purification, the Annunciation, the Nativity and the Dormition. This testimony is cited by Pope Pius XII in the Bull of the definition of the Assumption.[17]

In the West as in the East the feast celebrated on August 15 recalled the death of Mary and her entrance into glory. The bodily assumption was understood because the aforementioned oration "Veneranda" was said at the opening of the procession on the feast of the Dormition. It was placed there by Pope Sergius and is understood to refer to Mary's entrance into glory. For centuries this oration was found in the liturgy and until the latest revision after the Second Vatican Council was found in the Dominican and Carmelite missals. It is no longer used in the liturgy today,

---

[14]Jugie, *Op.cit.*, 195.

[15]Galot, J., *Op.cit.*, 175.

[16]Everett, L., O.SS.R., "Mary's Death and Bodily Assumption", in *Mariology*, 2 (1957) 480.

[17]*MD*, 70

perhaps because it refers explicitly to Mary's death which is not the object of the definition of the Assumption or of the feast. Already in the eighth century the feast is called the Assumption in the Gregorian Sacramentary that was sent by Pope Adrian I (772-795) to the Emperor Charlemagne. Later Pope Leo IV (847-855) decreed that a vigil and an octave be added. From Rome the feast found its way into other parts of Italy, France, England, Spain and Germany.[18]

The feast of the Assumption, however, received a setback in the West in the ninth century, something that never happened in the East, when uncertainty arose as to whether the feast included the bodily assumption of Mary. The doubt arose when the Abbot of Corbie, Paschase Radbert (d.865) published a spurious letter which he attributed to St. Jerome that spread false rumors about the bodily assumption of Mary. He does not deny the Assumption, but calls it into doubt, although admitting the incorruptibility of her body. He thought it ill-advised to accept the Assumption as certain in the absence of scriptural and traditional data. Unfortunately, part of the letter entered the readings of the Breviary. Doubts about the bodily assumption were multiplied when a monk Usuard by name (d. about 875), published his Martyrology that was used extensively in many monasteries and cathedral chapters from the ninth to the sixteenth century. In reference to the Assumption he said that the Church preferred pious ignorance to frivolous and apocryphal stories. The consequences of these doubts raised in learned circles checked the devotion of our Lady of the Assumption until about the middle of the thirteenth century when it became strong again, upheld not only in the liturgy but mainly by the great doctors, especially St. Albert the Great, St. Thomas Aquinas, and St. Bonaventure. Nevertheless, it was only in the sixteenth century that the doubt expressed by Usuard was stricken from the Martyrology, and that Pope Pius V removed the Pseudo-Jerome reading of Radbert from the divine office.

[18]*Ibid.,* 52.

In the same century the word Dormition was abandoned and emphasis placed on the word Assumption. Thus, the feast of Mary's bodily Assumption celebrated on August 15 became the greatest of the Marian feasts in the West and one of the most important of the liturgical year. A great theologian of that time, Suarez (d.1617) could write: "It is in some sort the feast that is proper to the holy virgin. Among all her feasts it has a quite special excellence, because it presents to us the glory, the reward and the triumph of the all Holy Virgin."[19]

After the solemn definition of the dogma in 1950 the Church celebrated the feast of the Assumption as a double first class feast with an octave and preceded by a vigil of fast and abstinence. With the latest reform mandated by the Second Vatican Council, the feast of the Assumption enjoys the highest rank. It is a Solemnity with a vigil Mass, but the fast and abstinence have been abolished, and the octave day is rightly honored with the feast of the Queenship of Mary. The object of the feast is that of the definition, namely that the whole person of Mary is in glory. In many parts of rural Europe the Assumption feast is our Lady's day in harvest time and celebrated with processions through the fields.

Outside the Roman Catholic Church the Orthodox honor August 15 with the feast of the Dormition. The bodily assumption of Mary is clearly affirmed in the hymns of the day.[20] The Anglican Church also celebrates Mary the Virgin feast on August 15 and the day is equally honored in the Calvinist community of Taizé.[21]

---

[19]Suarez, S.J. De Religione in *Opera,* ed. Vives, t.XIII, 283. cf. J. Duhr, *Op.cit.* 54.

[20]Ware, Timothy, *The Orthodox Church,* (1963) 263.

[21]Thurian, Max, brother of Taizé, writing about the ancient feast of August 15 has this to say: "Protestants believe that she [Mary] died, entered into heaven and awaits the resurrection like any other Christian. None the less, it does appear that in the spirit of ecumenical understanding and without any doctrinal confusion, we could all keep the same day of Mary's 'falling asleep' whatever may be the doctrine of this mystery which in faith we hold." cf. *Mary, Mother of the Lord, Figure of The Church,* (1963), London, 188.

Fuller, Reginald, Anglican scholar, who does not accept the dogma of the Assumption, in reference to the feast of August 15 writes: "We commemorate

In conclusion, the liturgical celebration of the Assumption in the East and the West is a proof and testimony that the faithful and their pastors have believed that God revealed that the whole person of Mary is in glory with Christ. It is a belief going back over at least fourteen centuries. The silence of the first centuries is not a sign that God did not reveal the Assumption to the Apostles. It only shows that this truth hidden in the deposit of faith did not immediately come to the explicit knowledge of the people. This explicit faith appeared once the early Church came to realize and appreciate that the revered mother of Jesus was joined in a hidden way with him in the same decree of predestination. Then, and only then, could the Church begin to publicly celebrate under the guidance of the magisterium the feast of the Assumption.

the apostles as martyrs although their martyrdoms are not related in the New Testament, and we believe with the Apocalypse that they are now praising God with angels and archangels and with the whole company of heaven. So why should we not believe that at her death our Lady was taken into heaven, and express our veneration for her by saying in poetry that she was given a place "next to her dear son?" "The Role of Mary in Anglicanism," his review of John de Satgé's book *Down to Earth in Worship,* 51 (1977) 223.

Chapter Five
Theological Arguments
for the Assumption

AS WE APPROACH the theological arguments and the support they offer for the dogma of the Assumption we are curious to know whether the theologians of the first part of this century had any influence on the papal decision. And if they did, whether they were the principal motivators behind the definition.

There is no doubt that in the years just prior to the papal definition the theologians worked vigorously to determine whether or not the doctrine of the Assumption was definable. The Pope asked for special studies. National and International Mariological Congresses were held. University faculties dedicated much of their time and some of their eminent members to study the question. Individual theologians took up the discussion. Various opinions appeared in periodicals. Controversies broke out. One of the strongest voices against the definition was the prominent patrologist Berthold Altaner. He argued from the lack of historical tradition and did not believe the Assumption to be definable. It was stated in rebuttal that the Assumption is not a subject of historical tradition but of dogmatic tradition.[1] History might prove that Mary died and was buried. It could never prove her resurrection or entrance into heaven. For her assumption cannot be known by natural reason. It is an event, a reality, but a mystery that

[1]Filograssi, I., S.J., "Theologia Catholica et Assumptio B.V.M." in *Gregorianum*, 31 (1950) 323-360.

we can only know if God reveals it to us. Altaner's opposition was formidable and influential, but once the definition was made it must be said to his credit that he accepted it.

Pope Pius XII was aware of the objections to a definition yet he also knew that prominent theologians believed that the doctrine of the Assumption was definable. There is no doubt that their decisions helped to influence his thinking. And some surely contributed to the preparation of the papal Constitution of the definition. Yet, it was not their reasoning or their faith that determined his decision. Rather, as we know, it was the universal faith of all the faithful, among whom the theologians were included. And this faith, as we have recently seen, was manifested in the liturgical feast celebrated for centuries in the whole Church.

Yet, the importance of theologians and their reasoning should not be underestimated. The Pope was aware of the influential voice of theologians down through the centuries in teaching and upholding the doctrine of the Assumption.

In the twelfth century an anonymous treatise on the Assumption "ad interrogata" appeared. It is known as the Pseudo-Augustine tract because it was attributed to the saint, no doubt to give it prestige. It was an influential force in allaying doubts that had been raised in the Pseudo-Jerome letter of Abbot Radbert. It affirmed the Assumption of Mary on the grounds of the filial love of Jesus for his mother.

The Pseudo-Augustine tract, excellent for its times, was not cited as an authority by the Holy Father in the Bull of the definition, yet it was supported by the theologians who in the Middle Ages began in the West to penetrate more deeply the meaning of the Assumption and to show how harmonious the Assumption was with other revealed truths. As we shall see they sought to root their reasoning in Sacred Scripture and in the mystery of Christ.

Among the theologians in defense of the Assumption, some of them eminent doctors in the annals of the Church, the following are cited in the Bull of definition: Amadeus, bishop of Lausanne (d.1159), St. Anthony of Padua (d.1231), St. Thomas Aquinas (d.1274), St. Bonaventure (d.1274), and St. Bernardine of Siena (d.1444). To these are added influential writers of the Counter-Reformation, for example, St. Peter Canisius (d.1597), St. Robert Ballarmine (d.1621), St. Francis de Sales (d.1622), St. Alphonsus Liguori (1787), and Francis Suarez (1677).[2]

The Holy Father, after offering the testimony of the theologians, draws up two arguments that he makes his own. They have been elaborated in one way or another by the theologians, but in making them his own the Holy Father first bases them on Holy Scripture. He then develops them in relation to the mystery of Christ. It is always Christ who is the center of our faith, and it is because Mary is Mother of God that she is endowed with privileges of holiness, virginity and finally of bodily assumption into heaven. It is precisely her motherhood that is the reason of her assumption. All the beauty of Mary stems from her relationship to Christ, and is God's gift to her.

The first of these two arguments is of the moral order. It is the filial love of Jesus that demands she be with him in heaven. The second argument is founded on the association of Mary with Jesus in his mission to restore the human family to the friendship of God.

At this point someone might ask whether these are the only two theological arguments proposed in the Bull of the definition that the Pope makes his own. What of the Immaculate Conception? This also is one of the preferred arguments of the Holy Father, but it is not found with the other two that follow from the tradition of the theologians. They did not argue from the Immaculate Conception to the Assumption because in the earlier centuries it was not a dogma of the faith, and many of the scholastics did not admit it. We can understand their

[2]Balic, C., O.F.M., *Testimonia de Assumptione B.V.M. ex omnibus saeculis.* Rome (1948) 2 vols. Source for the testimony of many more theologians.

doubts today, because at that time they did not clearly perceive that Mary could be redeemed, so to speak, in advance, by being preserved from contracting original sin. The idea of a preservative or anticipatory redemption had not yet been elaborated. Moreover, the feast of the Immaculate Conception was not a universal feast of the Church until the late Middle Ages. Hence, the earlier theologians appealed to Mary's holiness and her sinlessness as reasons for her Assumption, rather than her Immaculate Conception. But by the time of the Bull of the dogma of the Assumption, the Immaculate Conception had already been declared a dogma of the Faith, and could be considered in relation to the Assumption. In fact, the Holy Father gives great weight to this argument expressing the strong bond that unites the two privileges. He brings this out in the beginning of the Constitution of the definition where he shows that it was the definition of the dogma of the Immaculate Conception that gave the great impetus to the Assumptionist movement in the Church in the last century.

With these observations in mind we turn our attention to the theological arguments the Pope made his own.[3]

The Filial Love of Jesus for Mary

It is clear from the Sacred Scriptures that Jesus had a unique love for his Mother. Concerning this love *Munificentissimus* states: "These [the Holy Scriptures] set the loving mother of God as it were before our very eyes as most intimately joined to her Divine Son and as always sharing his lot. Consequently, it seems impossible to think of her, the one who conceived Christ, brought him forth, nursed him with her milk, held him in her arms, and clasped him to her breast, as being apart from him in body, even though not in soul. Since our Redeemer is the son of

[3]Theologians add other arguments especially from the holiness and virginity of Mary. Cf. Friethoff, C., O.P., "The Dogmatic Definition of the Assumption", in *The Thomist,* 14 (1951) 46.

Mary, he could not do otherwise, as the perfect observer of God's law, than to honor not only his eternal Father, but also his most beloved Mother. And since it was within his power to grant her this great honor, to preserve her from the corruption of the tomb, we must believe that he really acted in this way."[4]

This moral argument might strike some as being sentimental and founded on Mediterranean piety, but it is based on a universal human relationship independent of national cultures, and receives added weight when it is realized that it concerns the filial love that flows from the heart of the Word made flesh. The love of Jesus for his mother is not the love of any ordinary man for his mother. Jesus, as Son of God according to his divine nature and son of Mary according to his human nature, is different—he is a divine person. His filial love is beyond our human understanding.

The second theological argument proposed by the Holy Father—that Mary is the associate of Christ—also finds its roots in the Sacred Scriptures, but it is made explicit only in the writings of the Patristic Fathers. Three times in the Bull of the definition there is a reference to the Eve-Mary comparison. This is always presented as an inference from Scripture and Tradition.[5] It was only after reflection on the Scriptures that the early Church Fathers would refer explicitly to Mary as the New Eve. The first was St. Justin (d.165), followed by St. Irenaeus, bishop of Lyons (d.202). The latter writes: "So also we find the Virgin Mary obedient, saying, 'I am the handmaid of the Lord, let what you have said be done to me.' Eve in contrast was disobedient, she did not obey, even while she was a virgin . . . So it was that the knot which Eve's disobedience had tied together was unravelled by the obedience of Mary. What the virgin Eve had bound fast by her refusal to believe, the Virgin Mary has unbound by her belief."[6]

---

[4]*MD*, 75-76.
[5]*Ibid.*, 72, 73, 76.
[6]Ad haereses, 3:22:4. trans by Mackenzie, Ross in *Marian Studies*, 29 (1978) 67.

This reasoning, which for some is rather complicated, is neatly summed up by the Holy Father in these words: "We must remember especially that, since the second century, the Virgin Mary has been designated by the Holy Fathers as the New Eve, who, although subject to the New Adam, is most intimately associated with Him in the struggle against the infernal foe which as foretold in the pro-toevangelium, would finally result in the most complete victory over sin and death which are always mentioned together in the writings of the Apostle to the Gentiles. Consequently, just as the glorious resurrection of Christ was an essential part and the final sign of this victory, so that struggle which was common to the Blessed Virgin and her divine Son should be brought to a close by the glorification of her virginal body, for the same Apostle says: "When this mortal thing hath put on immortality, then shall come to pass the saying that is written: Death is swallowed up in victory."[7]

Again, we call attention to the way the Holy Father appeals to Scripture.[8] "Just as a single offense brought condemnation to all men, so a single righteous act brought all men acquittal and life. Just as through one man's disobedience all became sinners, through one man's obedience all became just."[9] In other words, the first man, Adam, brought sin and death into the world, the second Adam, Christ, brought grace and life.

But Adam did not sin alone. Eve also cooperated in bringing death and sin into the world, and she shared with Adam his subsequent life, parenthood and punishment for sin. Now just as a woman cooperated in the original sin, so also a woman, Mary, the new Eve, cooperated with Christ, the new Adam, although subject to him, in conquering sin and death. It was by his passion, death and resurrection that Christ overcame sin and death. Now, according to Scripture Mary cooperated freely with Christ in his saving work. She did this not only by her consent to be his

[7]*MD,* 76.
[8]Gen. 3:15 and Rom. 5 and 6; 1 Cor. 15:12-26; 54-57.
[9]Rom. 5:18-19.

mother, but also by her faithful association with him during his whole life even unto the cross. But the victory of Christ was accomplished only by his resurrection and glorification in heaven. Therefore, complete victory for Mary would be attained only by her glorification at the side of Christ in heaven. In other words, Mary's role as the new Eve demands her bodily assumption into heaven.

The Immaculate Conception

The third argument that the Holy Father employed is drawn from the close bond between the Immaculate Conception and the Assumption. As we stated previously, he does not place this with the other two arguments that were first expounded by the theologians and doctors of the Church, and have a long tradition. He argues from the dogmatic truth of the Immaculate Conception that had been defined just a little less than a hundred years before. It is, nevertheless, a theological argument of the highest quality and deserves to be numbered along with the arguments from divine motherhood and the intimate association of Mary with Jesus in the redemption.

We can best present this argument by recalling the definition of the Immaculate Conception by Pius IX: "that the Blessed Virgin Mary, in the first instant of her conception, by a singular grace and privilege granted by Almighty God, in view of the merits of Jesus Christ, the Savior of the human race, was preserved free of all stain of original sin."[10]

With this doctrine before his eyes Pius XII sees in Mary's freedom from original sin a binding connection with her glorious entrance into heaven. He writes: "That privilege [Assumption] has shone forth in new radiance since Our predecessor of immortal memory, Pius IX, solemnly proclaimed the dogma of the loving Mother of God's Immaculate Conception. These two privileges are

[10]Ineffabilis Deus, in the *Acta Pii IX,* part L, Vol. 1, p. 615.

most closely bound to one another. Christ overcame sin and death by his own death, and one who through baptism has been born again in a supernatural way has conquered sin and death through the same Christ. Yet, according to the general rule, God does not will to grant to the just the full effect of the victory over death until the end of time has come. And so it is that the bodies of even the just are corrupted after death, and only on the last day will they be joined each to its own glorious soul.''

"Now God has willed that the Blessed Virgin Mary should be exempted from this general rule. She, by an entirely unique privilege, completely overcame sin by her Immaculate Conception, and as a result she was not subject to the law of remaining in the corruption of the grave, and she did not have to wait until the end of time for the redemption of her body.''[11]

The force of this argument seems to be that preserved from original sin in her conception, Mary was also preserved from its effect, corruption in the tomb. For, in the present economy of salvation it is sin that causes corruption. But since Mary is free from sin, and no other valid reason can be offered for the corruption of her body, she did not suffer disintegration. In other words, the Assumption of Mary is implied in her Immaculate Conception.

If we turn to theologians to ask how they evaluate these three arguments as proofs for the Assumption of Mary, we find various interpretations. Some claim that the Assumption is implicitly revealed in the motherhood of Mary. Others, more numerous it seems, find it implicitly revealed in Mary's role as the new Eve.[12] Finally, it has been stated by a few that there is a *necessary* bond between the Immaculate Conception and the Assumption.[13] All would agree, however, that these arguments at least show that it is

---

[11]*MD*, 66.

[12]Lonergan, B., S.J., "The Assumption and Theology" in *Collection*, (1967) 68-83.

[13]Roschini, F., O.S.M., "The Assumption and the Immaculate Conception", in *The Thomist*, 14 (1951) 65. He gives a list of theologians who held a necessary connection between the Assumption and the Immaculate Conception.

fitting (some say most fitting) that Mary be taken up into heaven. We cannot solve this problem, and prefer to follow the example of the Constitution that does not evaluate the probative force of the individual arguments.

Here we would rather point out that once one admits the Assumption as a revealed truth from other sources, then these arguments, especially when taken together show clearly that the Assumption is in perfect harmony with other Marian privileges and doctrines of the faith. For example, by her Immaculate Conception and holiness of life Mary is free from all sin. By her virginal motherhood she is preserved from the biblical punishment of bringing forth her child in sorrow and by her Assumption she is spared the corruption of the body of the tomb. To put it more succinctly the Assumption is the crown and fulfillment of the life of the Immaculate Virgin Mother of Jesus. It is a testimony to the wisdom and merciful love of God who predestined her to the fullness of perfection corresponding to the dignity befitting the Mother of God, and her role as the new Eve in the redemption of the human family. It is Mary's involvement in the mystery of Jesus that reveals her Assumption.

The Use of Scripture

The Church has in effect proclaimed its faith in the Assumption of our Lady for many centuries through its liturgy, and the words of homilists and theologians. The latter have demonstrated the harmony of this mystery with other Marian privileges and with the mystery of Christ. With respect for the foundation for this belief, the Constitution of the definition states forthrightly that "all proofs and considerations of the Holy Fathers and the theologians are based upon the Sacred Writings as their ultimate foundation."[14]

[14]*MD*, 75.

It points out how the Fathers used different texts. As regards the Old Testament they accommodated many passages to Mary, for example, psalms 44/45:10, 14-16; 131/132:8; Songs 3:6; 4:8; 6:9; Is 60:13.

Clearly distinct from these texts are two from the New Testament cited by the theologians in the East and the West. The first, "Rejoice O highly favored daughter, the Lord is with you, and blessed are you among women."[15] The second text (we shall refer to it later) is Revelation 12. "A great sign appeared in the sky, a woman clothed with the sun, with the moon under her feet and on her head a crown of twelve stars."

The Pope did not pass judgment on the use of Scripture by the theologians except to say they were rather free in their application of events and texts in the Scriptures to explain their belief in the Assumption. But this does not mean to say he had no personal judgment on the value of Scripture in reference to the Assumption. For, in two places he makes arguments from the sacred Word his own. The first is the promise of redemption expressed in Genesis 3:15.[16] The Pope believes that this passage foretells the struggle between the infernal foe and the new Adam and the new Eve that resulted in complete victory over sin and death. Although he gives the text a mariological interpretation, common enough, it does not follow that he holds the Assumption to be formally revealed there.

The second scriptural foundation for the Assumption, the Holy Father finds in the gospels. He does not specify any particular text but remarks how the New Testament stresses Mary's relationship to Jesus. She conceived him and gave him birth, nursed him, clasped him in her arms. And on his part Jesus was a true and obedient son who would honor his beloved mother as he honored his eternal Father. Jesus who had a unique relationship to his Father, whom he called Abba, surely had a unique relationship with his mother. "And since it was within his power to

[15]Lk. 1:28.
[16]Gen. 3:15.

grant her this great honor to preserve her from the corruption of the tomb, we must believe that he really acted in this way.''[17] Hence, both arguments that the Holy Father chose to make his own, the concept of Mary as the new Eve and that of the divine motherhood, are well founded in Scripture, and both involve Mary with Christ.

Scripture does not explicitly state that Mary has been assumed into heaven. But Scripture does express the unique intimate, inseparable union between Jesus and his mother on earth. Early Christians who studied and contemplated the gospel story realized this. Contemplating the close union between Jesus and Mary, they would wonder about this union after his resurrection. Would they not be led to believe that the inseparable union on earth be continued in heaven? Was it not imperative that after his Ascension Jesus would take his mother with him? Is not the Assumption a complement of the Ascension? The more we contemplate the union of Jesus and Mary, the more we see that the Assumption is revealed in the mystery of Jesus.

This seems to be the thought of the Holy Father. And it also calls to mind the words of St. John of the Cross that we need no new revelations from God since he has revealed everything in his Word. ''In giving us his Son, his only Word (for he possesses no other), he spoke everything to us at once in this sole Word—and he has no more to say.'' ''For this reason the Father could say to us: 'Behold him well, for in him you will uncover all these revelations already made, and many more'.''[18]

Is Mary the Woman in Revelation 12?

We would not do justice to a Scriptural foundation for the Assumption if we omitted a discussion of Revelation 12. It begins: ''A great sign appeared in the sky, a woman

[17]*MD,* 76.
[18]*Collected Works of St. John of the Cross,* trans. by K. Kavanaugh, O.C.D., O. Rodriguez, O.C.D., Ascent, Bk. 2, ch. 22, al. 1, p. 179.

clothed with the sun, with the moon under her feet, and on her head a crown of twelve stars." Today this chapter is frequently applied to Mary in heaven, even in the liturgy of the Church. It seems that the woman clothed in the sun seen by the seer in his vision is a symbol of a woman in glory. Is she a symbol of the Virgin Mary in glory? If she is, do we have here an explicit revelation of the Assumption?

Munificentissimus Deus calls attention to the Scholastics who used this text and recognized the woman of the Revelation as a figure of the Assumption.[19] No names are mentioned but we know from other sources that none of them is in the first rank of theologians.[20]

The Holy Father offers no personal interpretation of the text, much less an official one. It is interesting, however, that in a prayer to our Lady of the Assumption, which he composed and delivered publicly immediately after the proclamation of the dogma, he salutes Mary with the words:

> "We believe finally that in the glory where you reign clothed with the sun and crowned with stars, you are, after Jesus, the joy and gladness of all the angels and the saints."[21]

Putting aside the above interpretations and uses of the text from Revelation, we may ask who, in the mind of the writer of Revelation, is the woman clothed with the sun?

Shortly after the definition of the dogma it was believed by a few that one day without doubt this text would be considered the scriptural proof of the Assumption. To some the passage of scripture seemed an inspired commentary of the protoevangelium. "And I will put enmity between you and the woman, and between your offspring

[19]*MD*, 72.

[20]Balic, C., *Op.cit.* vol. 1.

[21]*Papal Teachings. Our Lady,* ed. by Monks of Solesmes, Daughters of St. Paul, Boston, 324.

and hers."[22] That is, God will send a woman as the enemy of the devil, and her offspring will conquer the evil one. But for a complete victory over him, the woman as well as her seed, the redeemer, must triumph over the devil. Where do we find the complete victory for the woman? The prophecy is complete, they say, in Revelation 12. Here the woman is Mary taken into heaven, triumphant over the evil one, the serpent of old.[23]

Most theologians and exegetes today would not agree with the preceding exegesis. For them the primary reference of Revelation 12 is that the woman is a figure of the people of God, that is, of Israel or the Church or both.[24]

However, there are other writers, John McHugh for example, who would interpret the woman in the collective sense, but would admit a secondary reference to Mary. "The woman in *Apoc.* 12 is therefore an ambivalent symbol. She certainly represents the people of God on earth, that is, the Jewish people and the faithful remnant, from whom Christ was born, and the Christian Church which is the mother of all who believe in Jesus. But she also symbolizes the heavenly Jerusalem which is our mother (Gal 26:7), mother of the Messiah and of all the faithful: she is the Church of the Old and the New Testament as existing in the foreordaining mind and will of God. She is not only the Church in history, but the people of God predestined in the city of God."[25]

After making these observations the writer goes on to consider the likelihood of a secondary reference to Mary. He reasons that Revelation 12 cannot be fully understood unless it is seen in relation with the fourth Gospel in which

[22]Gen. 3:15.

[23]For a list of writers who hold that Rev. 12 is a direct reference to Mary and an indirect reference to the Church, cf. Brown, R., etc. in *Mary in the New Testament,* 235, n.510.

[24]*Ibid.,* 231-232.

[25]McHugh, J., *The Mother of Jesus in the New Testament,* 425. For a list of other writers holding a double reference cf. Brown, R., etc., *Op.cit.,* 235.

Mary is presented as the mother of all whom Jesus loves, and by reason of her faith especially at Cana and Calvary, the model of all the disciples of Jesus. He states: ". . . when we look at the mother of Jesus as portrayed in John's gospel we find the archetypal symbol of Apocalypse 12 made concrete, practical and present in this world. For in the fourth Gospel the mother of Jesus is the prototype and exemplar of the Christian believer, and may therefore justly be called the archetype of the Church realized on earth. She is above all others the woman who went through torment as she saw Jesus born on Calvary (Apoc 12:2), who saw him taken up to God and to his throne (v.5), and who was later to witness the suffering of the rest of her children (v.17)."[26]

For McHugh, then, we have a primary reference to the faithful people of God of both dispensations, and a secondary reference to Mary in Revelation 12. The woman clothed with the sun is a symbol of the faithful remnant of Zion which became the nucleus of the Christian Church, and also a symbol of Mary. For in history Mary personifies the woman described in Revelation 12.[27]

Finally, there is another opinion that agrees that the primary reference is the Church, but is not sure of a secondary reference to Mary. In the words of the Task Force that presents this opinion: "A secondary reference to Mary in Revelation 12 remains possible but uncertain, so far as the intention of the seer himself is concerned. What is more certain is that his symbol of the woman who is the mother of the Messiah might well lend itself to Marian interpretation, once Marian interest developed in the later Christian community. And eventually when Revelation was placed in the same canon of Scripture with the Gospel of Luke and the Fourth Gospel, the various images of the virgin, the woman at the cross, and the woman who gave birth to the Messiah would reinforce each other."[28]

[26]*Ibid.,* 431.
[27]For other writers holding a double reference, cf. Brown, R., etc., *Op.cit.* 235.
[28]*Ibid.* 239.

We conclude that there is no consent, even among Catholics, in regard to the woman of Revelation. Perhaps with time and study a consensus will emerge. But even if the woman is a figure of Mary, it would still be necessary to show that there is a certain reference to the Assumption in the text. In the meantime, without making any categorical decision on the identity of the woman in the literal sense, the Church finds no problem in applying the text of Revelation in its liturgy in reference to the Assumption, for the expression "the woman clothed with the sun, with the moon beneath her feet, and a crown of twelve stars on her head" is an image that calls to mind Mary, the Mother of Jesus in glory.

Conclusion of the First Part

In the preceding study of the Constitution *Munificentissimus* we tried to emphasize the precise meaning of the dogma, and how it is a revealed truth hidden in the mystery of Jesus Christ, the Word made flesh. In doing this we hope to have remained faithful to the document which is a remarkable presentation of the reasons that guided Pope Pius XII to define the Assumption as a dogma of the faith. At the close of the Constitution he himself sums up the reasons for his decision:

The Universal Church, the faithful and their bishops, have professed their faith in the Assumption of Mary as a revealed truth over the course of centuries. This truth is based on the Sacred Scripture. It is rooted in the minds of the faithful. It is approved and professed in the liturgy from remote times. It is completely in harmony with other revealed truths. It has been expounded and explained magnificently in the writings and wisdom of the theologians. Therefore, it is opportune to define it.[29]

But notice once again, the importance of the Scriptures. Take away the place given to Mary in the life of Christ as

[29]*MD*, 76-77.

portrayed in Scripture and you destroy the foundation for the Assumption of Mary. Without Jesus the Virgin Mary is unintelligible. She is what she is because she is Mother of Jesus and his associate in the work of redemption. It is her relation to Christ as Mother that explains why she is immaculate and virginal, and why she is now with him in glory. She shared in his redemptive mission on earth, and she continues now in heaven to share that mission with him until all the world is lifted up to the Father on the last day. This is the divine plan.[30]

This was all said most beautifully by St. Germanus, Patriarch of Constantinople in the eighth century: "It is time . . . to take you to be with me, you, my mother. Just as you filled the earth and its people with joy, so now you shall bring joy to the heavens, bring happiness to the mansions of my Father . . . Where I am there is light eternal, joy without compare, a palace without equal, a city safe from ruin. And so where I am, you shall also be. Mother inseparable in her inseparable Son."[31]

[30]*Cultus Marialis,* 25. Pope Paul VI emphasizes the same truth in his desire for a renewal of Marian devotion. "In the Virgin Mary everything is relative to Christ and dependent upon him. With Christ in mind God the Father chose her from all eternity to be the all holy Mother and adorned her with gifts of the Spirit granted to no one else. Certainly geniune Christian piety has never failed to highlight the Virgin's indissoluble link and essential relationship to the divine Savior." trans. in *The Pope Speaks,* 19 (1974) 65.

[31]Hom. 2 in Dorm. *PG,* 98, 361A.

Part Two
The Assumption in the Mystery
of the Church.

Chapter Six
The Assumption and
the Pilgrim Church

IN THE PRECEDING part one truth stands out clearly. There is an inseparable union between Jesus and Mary. It began at the Incarnation and continues without end. For rising from the dead and ascending into heaven where he reigns as King of the Universe Jesus has taken up his mother to be at his side. She is the first fruits of his redemption. We call her the Lady of the Assumption, the Queen of heaven. This has been the faith of the Church for centuries and is now made secure by the solemn definition of the Church.

In this part we wish to contemplate more deeply this mystery of the Assumption; not the definition, not the act by which Mary's body and soul was taken up, but the definitive state of glory that Mary enjoys, that is, her fullness of life. We intend to contemplate the glorious Virgin not in herself, but in her relationship with others. She is not glorified in isolation.

In her heavenly state she enjoys a unique union with the Blessed Trinity and a special relationship with the Church. It is the Assumption-Church relationship that interests us because it has been said that the proclamation of the dogma of the Assumption was not so much a glorification of Mary as a glorification of the Church. However, a brief word about the Assumption and the Blessed Trinity is in order.

Assumption-Blessed Trinity

In her heavenly state Mary is in communion with the Blessed Trinity. She is the highly favored daughter of the Father whom he had predestined before all other women to be the mother of his son incarnate. She is the bride of the Father. The Second Vatican Council chooses to call her daughter rather than bride, but bride of the Father is also suitable. For this metaphor symbolizes the mystical marriage of the Father with Mary . . . a union begun at the Immaculate Conception and perfected by her Assumption into glory.

In heaven there is also a unique relation with the Son made man. If Jesus had a unique relationship with his Father whom he called Abba, he certainly had a unique relationship with his mother, Mary. As we have seen in the first section it is an intimacy made more perfect once she was taken up to heaven, because now her faith has turned to vision.

Finally there is Mary's relationship with the Holy Spirit. It began on earth at the moment of her conception when the Holy Spirit dwelt within her and sanctified her whole being. All her life she would be the temple of the Holy Spirit, who found her always responsive to his will. And now that she has been taken up into heaven who can fathom the communion of the Holy Spirit with Mary?

Confronted with such profound mysteries we are almost inarticulate and sense that only someone led by the Spirit in a special way and who therefore enjoys divine secrets can penetrate the mystical union of Mary with the Trinity, to whom she owes everything. This much we will say. Surely, in heaven Mary is always attentive to the Father, Son and Holy Spirit whom she sees in blissful vision, and with whom she is united in a bond of unbreakable love. She is the perfect Christian, the bride-mother, the preeminent member of the Church caught up in the consuming fire of God.

Assumption-Church

But if Mary is close to the Blessed Trinity she is also close to the Church, because she is a member, and representative of the Church. So, let us look more closely at the Assumption-Church relationship. Before the definition of the Assumption many of us did not see clearly the relation of this truth to the Church. We isolated the privilege of Mary's heavenly glory from the overall role of Mary in the plan of salvation. Intent on penetrating more deeply the Assumption as the normal effect and crown of her immaculate, virginal motherhood, and her role as the new Eve we sought to prove the fittingness of the Assumption for one who was so intimately united with Christ. Consequently, some of us failed to ponder the Assumption as the model and pattern of all the elect. Even the Bull of the definition does not explicitly reflect on the Assumption-Church relationship. However, in fairness it should be said that it expressed the hope that one of the benefits of the definition would be to lead people to think of their own resurrection.

This hope has not been in vain, for in the course of time and the help of theologians we have come to ponder the Assumption-Church relationship, and now see more clearly its importance to the Church. But before we examine this mystery, there is need to determine what we mean by Church. For this, too, is a mystery that defies a comprehensive definition since it is a divine reality that escapes the grasp of human thought and language. It is always open to new and greater exploration. Here we limit our consideration to the Church as the people of God living in three different phases of life, that is, the Church militant, suffering and triumphant. This mode of expression once common has given way to the more appropriate language of the Second Vatican Council that describes the one Church as pilgrim, suffering and heavenly, namely the Church of the faithful here on earth, the souls in purgatory and the saints in heaven.[1]

Beginning with the pilgrim Church we shall consider each phase in relation to the Assumption. But a question immediately comes to mind: Who are the members of the pilgrim Church? Pope Paul VI can help us here. In one of his many homilies delivered after the Council he addressed this question to the people and gave the following answer: "A person can belong to the Church in reality, or *in voto* virtually, by desire (as catechumens) or even by properly directing a life that may be deprived of any explicit knowledge of Christianity, but that is, because of the person's moral uprightness, open to a mysterious mercy of God. That mercy can link to mankind saved by Christ, and therefore to the Church, all the immense multitudes of human beings 'who sit in the shadow of death,' but who are themselves created and loved by the divine goodness."[2] Only a sin that is expressly directed against belonging to the Church: heresy, schism, apostasy or that implies separation from the community, which means excommunication interrupts adherence to the Church. At the same time it is well to remember that anyone who does not persevere in charity is not saved, although he remains in the body of the Church.

In the following story we find a concrete application of this teaching. On February 6, 1943 during World War II an

[1] *LG,* 49, 50. These three conditions of the Church form the one Mystical body of Christ.

[2] *The Pope Speaks,* 11 (1966) 374. Cf. *LG,* 14: "They are fully incorporated in to the society of the Church, who, possessing the Spirit of Christ, accept her entire system and all means of salvation given to her, and through union with her visible structure are joined to Christ, who rules her through the Supreme Pontiff and the bishops."

". . . men who believe in Christ and have been properly baptized (in communities separated from full communion with the Catholic Church) are brought into a certain though imperfect communion with the Catholic Church." Second Vatican Council, *Decree on Ecumenism,* 3.

American troopship, the Dorchester, was torpedoed near Greenland and began to sink. When four young soldiers seeking to abandon the ship turned up without life jackets, four chaplains, a Catholic, a Jew and two Protestants took theirs off and gave them to the four servicemen. Then clasping hands and praying they went down with the ship. All were pilgrims on their last journey to the Father. At least one was not baptized, yet all were open to the mysterious mercy of the one true God in whom they believed and trusted. We can believe that in God's hidden Providence all four entered into the Kingdom, and knowingly or unknowingly, through the grace of Christ, the one mediator for all. And in some way all were linked to the one Church.

Keeping in mind the different ways one can be united to the pilgrim Church or linked with it, we press on to consider the relation between Mary assumed into heaven and the pilgrim Church. But let us understand clearly this is only one segment of the Mary-Church relationship, an early Christian theme that has been pondered more deeply since the definition of the Assumption. For centuries Mary and the Church have been constantly associated. Their links are numerous and close. Neither are they external and arbitrary but internal and essential. One might say they "are one single unique mystery." One helps to explain the other.[3] For example, both are called the new Eve. Mary enjoys the title because by her faith and obedience she cooperated with Christ, in a subordinate way, in the work of salvation. So also the Church by its faith and obedience, following the example of Mary cooperates in bringing its members to salvation. Again, both are called the Ark of the Covenant, the Gate of heaven, the bride of Christ, etc. "Both are—after Christ—the dwelling place of wisdom, and even wisdom herself, both are "a new world" and a prodigious creation, both rest in the shadow of Christ.[4] Finally, both are called Virgin Mother as we shall see.

[3] de Lubac, H., S.J., *The Splendour of the Church,* (1956) 200.
[4] *Ibid.*

How explain this interchange of titles? One reason is that the early Church saw in Mary the perfect Christian, the concrete model, the ideal for all the faithful. Followers of Christ contemplated Mary and saw in her what the Church should be. So, from the time of St. Ambrose (d.397) in the late fourth century Mary is the model, the type, the exemplar of the Church. This led to an ample and fruitful contemplation of Mary and the Church. In our time we find it beautifully expressed in the Second Vatican Council that draws on tradition and refers to Mary as the type, model and image of the Church.[5] These are not arbitrary titles. They tell us the Church has already begun to exist in Mary. She is a concrete personal member of the Church in which all other members can see their exemplar. In the words of a recent book: "When we call Mary 'type or symbol or archetype' of the Church, we regard her not as an arbitrary figure of the Church, but as the living and perfect exemplar of the Church, of what it means to be a member of Christ. The choice of Mary as type of the Church is not a mere human convention; she was chosen by God to be perfect model of the Church of which she is herself a member, first of the followers of Jesus."[6]

Every member of the Church is called to contemplate our Lady; to imitate her faith, hope and love; and even to see in her an exemplar of virginity and motherhood. For, just as Mary is the mother who brought forth Christ, so the Church as mother brings forth in baptism Christ in new born Christians. And just as Mary as a virgin brings forth Christ, so the Church as virgin possesses the integrity of the fullness of faith. The title "the virgin Church" recalls to mind that the Church received the faith from Christ, her bridegroom, and as a true bride possesses the truth in its integrity and will never be corrupted by going into error. This is explained beautifully by the Benedictine Honorius of Autun (d.1136): "The glorious Virgin Mary stands for the Church, who is also both virgin and mother. She is

[5]*LG,* 63.
[6]Carroll, E., O. Carm., *Understanding the Mother of Jesus,* (1979) 28.

mother because every day she presents God with new sons in baptism, being made fruitful by the Holy Spirit. At the same time she is virgin because she does not allow herself to be in any way corrupted by the defilement of heresy, preserving inviolate the integrity of the faith. In the same way Mary was mother in bringing forth Jesus and virgin in remaining intact after bearing him.''[7]

The Mary-Church theme so popular in tradition is still recommended to the faithful for contemplation and inspiration. In his letter on Marian devotion Pope Paul VI explains the place of Mary in the renewed liturgy of the Church, and points out the varied relations existing between the Mother of Christ and the Church. For example, there are texts which recognize in the Virgin's Immaculate Conception the beginning of the Church, the spotless Bride of Christ. This thought is developed in the preface of the feast.

This introduction to our Assumption-pilgrim Church theme may seem rather long, but we think it necessary to understand that this relation is not arbitrary or insignificant. It is a relation chosen by God, who willed that Mary be the model of his Church. And this finds its fulfillment in her heavenly glory. By reason of her Assumption Mary enjoys the fullness of glory that is the ultimate destiny of the pilgrim Church. She is the model and type to which the Church is being formed. Her Assumption is a constant reminder that life does not cease with death of the body, it is only changed, and that one day everyone who dies in the friendship of God, will rise body and soul to enter into glory. The article of the creed "we believe in the resurrection of the dead" is already fulfilled in Mary. Her Assumption is a guarantee of the Church's assumption. As Karl Rahner writes: "The Church looks on high and greets in Mary her own type and model, her own future in the resurrection of the body."[8] And the Second Vatican Council affirms the same truth with these words: "in the bodily and

[7]*Sigillum Beatae Mariae,* PL, 172, 499, quoted by de Lubac, *Op.cit.,* 201.
[8]Rahner, Karl, S.J., *Mary Mother of the Lord.* (1963) 92.

spiritual glory which she possesses in heaven, the Mother of Jesus continues in this present world as the image and first flowering of the Church as she is to be perfected in the world to come.''[9] Mary's glorification is the glorification of the Church, a sign of hope and consolation for all pilgrims. She is the first member of the Church to reach the fullness of glory, and to be perfectly conformed to Christ, the Redeemer. Where she is, the Church will one day be! In the words of the Preface of the feast of the Assumption: "Today the virgin Mother of God was taken up into heaven to be the beginning and the pattern of the Church in its perfection, and a sign of hope and comfort for your people on their pilgrim way."

Intercession

As the Church contemplates its own final glory in the mystery of the Assumption, it comes to realize that in glory Mary is more than a model, the first flowering of the Church. She is a concerned mother, who actively intercedes for its salvation. In heaven she cares for the pilgrim Church, and the Church believes this and responds with heartfelt devotion. There is, therefore, a twofold activity to be considered here: Mary's intercession and the Church's devotion. These are two aspects of the Assumption-pilgrim Church relationship. Our concern here is with Mary's intercession. In the following chapter we shall consider the Church's response.

When we think of Mary's intercession for us we are aware that she is present to the Church. Glorified in heaven, no longer bound by the spatio-temporal limits of this world, she is, like the Lord Jesus, invisible, but none the less present. Her intercession is exercised through explicit prayer and interpretative prayer. The former is simply her beseeching the Lord to grant our needs. Interpretative prayer refers to her heavenly influence which comes from her participation in the mission of Christ while

[9]*LG,* 68.

she was on earth. In our study we presuppose her cooperative role with Christ on earth, and concentrate on her explicit prayer. Belief in this intercession is of the greatest importance for Marian devotion, for it is the motive and foundation of all prayer that is addressed to her. If the faithful did not believe she had some heavenly power or influence they would not pray to her.

But speaking of her heavenly intercession brings up the very thorny question of mediation that Catholics accept without difficulty but that has caused no end of controversy with other Christians. Indeed, for many Protestants the intercession of Mary (and for that matter of the saints) is opposed to the Lordship of Christ. Yet, if there is no mediation on Mary's part, there is no intercession. Hence, the need here to clarify the meaning of mediation.

There is no doubt that there is only one mediator between God and all people, Jesus the Lord.[10] The Second Vatican Council emphasizes this truth lest there be any doubt in the minds of those who wish to know the true Catholic faith. Christ alone reconciles us to the Father by his death and resurrection. No other agent reconciles us with God, and there is no other who is a coequal mediator or redeemer with him. He stands alone as the one who brings peace between heaven and earth.

If this is so, how can we speak of other mediators or in the case of Mary, a mediatrix? The presence of a sole mediator does not rule out others who may cooperate with Christ, not as equals, not as necessary but in subordinate and dependent roles. As St. Thomas states: "There is no reason why certain others should not be called in a certain way mediators between God and man, that is to say in so far as they cooperate by predisposing the ministering in the union of man with God."[11] To use human beings to save other human beings does not take power away from God, but rather shows that he has power to use creatures to obtain his end.

It is in this sense that Mary is called a mediatrix. The

[10] 1 Tim. 2:5.
[11] *Summa Theologica*, III, q.26, a.2.

mother of Jesus is inseparably joined to her son's saving work.[12] She exercised the office of mediation in so far as she cooperated actively in the Incarnation of the Word, thereby becoming not only the mother of Jesus, the Redeemer, but also the spiritual mother of all whom he would redeem. During his ministry she cooperated with him as his first and most perfect disciple. She showed the depths of her discipleship when she stood beneath the Cross and suffered in her heart what Jesus suffered in his body and spirit. And now taken up into heaven she is still associated with him, interceding by her prayers for the completion of the work of salvation. In other words, in her own subordinate way, willed by the Father, she ministers to Christ and the Church at the Incarnation, during his life, at the foot of the Cross, and now in heaven. Just as Eve had her place in the fall of the human race, so Mary has her place as the new Eve in the restoration of all people to God's friendship. And just as ministers of the Church share the priesthood of Christ and cooperate in the work of redemption, so Mary was chosen by God to cooperate in the work of redemption by first consenting to the Incarnation, and now by her intercession in heaven. In fact we should never forget that "each of us is responsible for the salvation of his brethren and can and must intercede for them with prayer and sacrifice and aid."[13] The following declaration of the Council, therefore, comes as no surprise: ". . . the Blessed Virgin Mary is invoked by the Church under the title of Advocate, Auxiliatrix, and Mediatrix. These, however, are to be so understood that they neither take away from nor add anything to the dignity and efficacy of Christ the one mediator."[14]

Unfortunately, these titles have not always been clearly understood. Mary's heavenly ministry is not to be conceived as if she were the door that must be opened before we meet Christ, or the bridge to be crossed before we en-

[12]*LG*, 55-59.
[13]Rahner, *Op.cit.*, 31.
[14]*LG*, 2.

counter him. No. We enter directly into union with the Lord through the Spirit, and without doubt many Christians meet Christ daily in their prayer and work without even a thought of our Lady in heaven. By intercession we understand, as mentioned above, that in the first place Mary in her glorious Assumption prays for us, as do all the saints in heaven who are one with Christ and one with us through the Spirit. Her intercession assists us as we enter into immediate communion with Christ. We have no experience of how Mary and the saints pray except that living in communion with the Blessed Trinity in unending joy, and loving us, they pray for our entrance into glory.

It is lamentable that in the history of the people of God devotion to Mary sometimes got out of hand. For example, Mary was often pictured as the mother of mercy in opposition to Christ, the severe judge. The impression was given that one had to pray to Mary in order to temper the severity of the Lord. This distortion occurred especially in the Middle Ages when a very personal, affective devotion to Mary became prevalent. Most of the poor people who frequented the parish churches could not read, and depended on the paintings and frescoes on the walls of the churches for much of their instructions in the faith. In these Christ was on many occasions portrayed as the severe judge and Mary as the merciful mother pleading with her son for our salvation. Sometimes Mary was portrayed alone as mother of mercy leading some, perhaps, to conclude that she alone could save them. Even the Last Judgment scene of Michelangelo in the Sistine Chapel has led some to come away with the misguided impression that Jesus is a severe, unrelenting judge to be feared. Hence, the need of a merciful mother. In our time we have met people who have been brought up from childhood to fear the punishment of the Lord. Their whole life has been motivated not by love of God but by fear of judgment. In such misunderstanding it is not surprising that they would turn to Mary as their only hope pitting her mercy against the justice of the Lord. Pope Paul VI only a few years ago found it necessary to correct such a distorted devotion. In a homily on the feast of the Assumption in 1964 in the parish church of Castel Gandolfo he felt constrained to say: "There are some naive minds that regard our Lady as more merciful than the Lord. Through childish judgment, they reach the conclusion that the Lord is more severe than she, and that we need to have recourse to our Lady because otherwise the Lord will punish us. It is true that Our Lady is entrusted with the very special office of interceding for us, but the source of all goodness is the Lord. Christ is the one mediator, the one font of grace."[15]

Mary's intercession, then, cannot be placed on the same level as that of Christ our Savior, who always intercedes for us. Her mediation is subordinate, it is that of a concerned mother for the safety of her children. She cares for us, because it is first of all God who cares for us. In heaven, then, she prays for us. It is difficult to understand why some devout Christians, who believe in life after death, reject Mary's intercessory role. They think it quite normal to ask their friends to pray for them, but not Mary. Is it not true that in Christian churches, especially on Sunday, people gather and not only praise and give thanks to the Lord, but offer prayers for one another, for the elderly, the sick, the poor, for everyone in need? Surely, in this they follow the example of St. Paul who exhorted the faithful to "pray constantly and attentively for all in the holy company. Pray for me that God may put his words on my lips, that I may courageously make known the mystery of the gospel."[16]

If we believe in the intercessory value of the prayers of the pilgrim Church, why do we doubt the power of the intercession of the Virgin Mary and the saints in the heavenly Church? After all, they are our friends too, united securely in the same bond of love in Christ. We are one in Christ. In heaven as on earth they love us and pray that one day we

---

[15] *The Pope Speaks,* 10 (1964) 57. Cf. Marialis cultus, 38. Incorrect attitudes of piety toward Mary are scored.

[16] Ep. 6:18-19, Cf. Col. 4:2-4.

will be with them. Living in the eternal Kingdom enjoying the vision and love of God, they certainly pray that we will join them. This is a belief not only of Orthodox and Roman Catholics, but of many non-Catholics. One evangelical Christian who finds no difficulty in admitting the subordinate mediation of Mary and the saints—providing it finds its efficacy in Christ the one mediator—writes: "It is for this reason that Protestants may, with no violence to their fundamental convictions, ally themselves with the supplication of the mother of God, as well as with those of such of their contemporaries as they wish, for the furtherance of their efforts in the gospel. And what is true of the mother of God is true of all the saints."[17]

Calvin also admitted the intercession of saints that would not interfere with the rights of the One Intercessor. And one theologian brought up in the Calvinist tradition states: "And when I pray, 'Blessed mother of Christ our Lord guard me with your protection, for I know you pray without ceasing for me', I know that Mary's ministry and her prayer are that I may come to Christ and find her God and mine."[18] Finally, a brother of the religious community of Taizé, writing in the same tradition states: "The Reformed Church in general admits that the dead pray, and pray for us, although the Reformers when they speak of these matters, stress the limitations of these prayers more than they take pleasure in pointing out the grace they represent."[19]

The Catholic Church on the contrary, both in the East and the West takes great pleasure in recalling Mary's intercession. This tradition goes back to the prayer "We fly to thy patronage, O holy mother of God" that began in the East, and is given eloquent testimony by the Eastern homilists of the seventh and eighth centuries. Listen to the

[17]de Satgé, J., *Down to Earth,* (1976) 119.

[18]Mackensie, Ross, "Calvin and the Calvinists on Mary", 18. Paper given at the Ecumenical Society of the Blessed Virgin Mary, Wash. D.C., (1980).

[19]Emery, Pierre Yves, *The Communion of Saints,* trans. P.J. and M. Watson, London (1966) 107.

expression of faith in the words of St. Germanus of Constantinople: "No one is redeemed unless through you, O mother of God. You are always heard, because God always listens to his true and sinless Mother . . . The entire Christian family, trusting completely in you commits its prayers to God through you."[20] Then too, the Byzantine liturgy celebrated also in the Orthodox Church bears witness to faith in her intercession. On the feast of the Assumption the faithful pray: "In giving birth thou didst preserve thy virginity, in thy Falling asleep thou hast not forsaken the world, O mother of God. Thou hast passed into life, thou art the mother of God, and through thine intercession dost deliver our souls from death."[21] It should be noticed that in the East the basis for intercession is the divine motherhood. Jesus will listen to his mother. That Mary is also our spiritual mother is only implied. But when you turn to the West that has acknowledged Mary's intercession for centuries, the reason for her intercession is not only her divine motherhood but her spiritual motherhood. In recent years there is ample papal teaching that proclaims Mary as our spiritual mother and emphasizes her heavenly intercession for the Church. But already in the Middle Ages this is the testimony of Amadeus, bishop of Lausanne. After extolling Mary's Assumption into heaven at the right hand of Christ the King he closes his homily with this thought:

"Then coming down to the human race in ineffable charity and turning upon us those eyes of pity with which heaven is brightened, she lifts her prayer alike for clergy, for the people of either sex, for the living and for the departed. Here from heaven is the glorious Virgin most powerful in prayer, driving away every hurtful thing and bestowing what is good, and she grants to all who pray to

[20]Hom. 2 Dorm. *PG,* 98, 349.

[21]Gumbinger, Cuthbert, O.F.M. Cap., "Mary in the Eastern Liturgies", in *Mariology,* I, (1954) 202. St. Bernard, (d.1153) wrote four sermons for the feast of the Assumption. He speaks eloquently of Mary's intercession, although he never openly mentions the bodily Assumption. Cf. Graef, Hilda, *Mary,* Vol. 1, (1963) 235-241.

her from the heart her protection for this present life and for that to come.''

''For remembering for what purpose she was made the Mother of the Redeemer, most willingly she gathers up the sinner's prayers and pleads with her Son for all the guilt of those who are penitent. Surely she will gain what she wishes, the dear Mother through whose chaste womb the Word of God came to us, the sin offering of the world, to wash away with his own blood the bond of original sin, Jesus Christ our Lord, who lives and reigns with God the Father in the unity of the Holy Spirit, God for ever and ever. Amen.''[22]

The liturgy of the Roman rite in Eucharistic Prayer I, in use already in the fifth century, testifies to Mary's intercession: ''In union with the whole Church we honor Mary, the ever virgin mother of Jesus Christ our Lord and God . . . and all the saints. May their merits and prayers gain your constant help and protection. Through Christ our Lord. Amen.'' And in the most recent votive Mass of Mary, Mother of the Church, we pray in the preface: ''Raised to the glory of heaven she cares for the Pilgrim Church with a mother's love following its progress homeward until the day of the Lord dawns in splendor.'' To this we may add the words of the prayer of Pope Pius XII written for the occasion of the definition of the Assumption: ''We are inspired by the certainty that your eyes, which wept over the earth watered by the blood of Jesus, are yet turned toward this world, held in the clutches of wars, persecution, oppression of the just and the weak.''[23]

There is an incident in the life of St. Therese of Lisieux that sheds some light on the mystery of our Lady's intercession. From childhood her thoughts were often about heaven, and as death drew near at the early age of twenty-four, she who had called her life a vocation of love in the

---

[22]*Magnificat, Homilies in Praise of the B.V.M.,* Cistercian Publication Inc., Kalamazoo, Mich. (1979) Hom. VII, 127-128.

[23]*Papal Teachings, Our Lady,* ed, by Monks of Solemnes, trans. Daughters of St. Paul, 324.

heart of the Church continued to ponder its mystery. She promised her sisters that in heaven she would not forget the Church. For, in heaven her mission would begin, a mission to send roses, heavenly graces, to adorn the Church and to raise up souls for the Lord. In heaven she would pray and not rest until every soul redeemed by Christ was saved. This would not be impossible she believed, because just as in the bosom of the beatific vision the angels watch over us, so would she.[24]

St. Therese foresaw a personal mission of intercession in heaven for the Church. Does this not tell us something about the mission of all the saints, and especially about the mission of our Lady? Can we not see in the Assumption of Mary, the beginning of a unique mission to the whole Church on pilgrimage? Indeed we can, but it is only a part of the mission of Mary. Her whole life was and is a mission for all. She was called by the Father, who first loved us, to be the Mother of Jesus and the mother of the Church. Her mission is a maternal mission, a universal mission to all men and women. All the privileges granted to her were to fulfill this purpose. They were not only for her personal adornment. Her whole life was to minister to Christ, and with him, but subordinate to him, to minister to others. By her Assumption she actively intercedes for us. It is her Assumption that gives her spiritual motherhood its full efficacy. God in his freedom has given her this role which he honors. He wills to bring us to salvation through the maternal intercession of Mary. Therefore, in her heavenly glory she not only reminds the pilgrim Church what it will be one day; she not only offers hope and consolation, but by her intercession she calls on the Holy Spirit to lead the people of God to unity in Christ, and through Christ, to the Father. Only when all the elect are one body in Christ, in the heavenly Church, will her intercessory role be finished.

Finally, for those who seek a scriptural basis for Mary's

---

[24]*St. Therese of Lisieux. Her Last Conversations.* trans. John Clarke, O.C.D., (1979) 102.

intercession, let us say that the Church writers, especially the fathers of the Eastern Church found it in her divine motherhood. Her intimacy with our Lord that began on earth gives her prayer in heaven a special efficacy. The son will listen to his mother whom the Scriptures tell us was not only mother but intimate associate, faithful disciple. For example, at the wedding feast of Cana, Mary interceded for the young bride and groom about to be embarrassed because the wine at their wedding feast had run out. It is Mary who brings the plight of the couple to the attention of Jesus, and then instructs the waiters to do whatever he tells them. Influenced by his mother, Jesus changes the water into wine. What happened at Cana is an indication of the relation of Mary to Jesus that will continue in heaven. If Jesus listened to her on earth, he will certainly listen to her in heaven. By her Assumption she is in a glorified state that disposes her to exercise fully her unique motherly intercession. For, by her bodily presence in glory she still remains in solidarity with all men and women on earth. And by her intimate union with Jesus, free from all earthly restrictions, she is able to extend her intercession to all.[25] For these reasons the pilgrim Church full of confidence and trust raises its heart and voice to Mary daily: "Be with us now and at the hour of our death."

[25]*LG*, 62.

Chapter Seven
Devotion to Our Lady
of the Assumption

IN THE PRECEDING chapter we stated that in the Assumption-Church relationship there are two activities to be considered: Mary's intercession for the Church, and the Church's activity toward Our Lady of the Assumption. Having considered Mary's intercession we turn now to contemplate the pilgrim Church's relation to Mary in glory. Before doing this it is necessary to recall that this relationship, which is really one of devotion on the part of the Church, is only one aspect of a more general Marian devotion. And a few words about this general devotion are in order.

It is a known fact that the Church honors and venerates the Virgin Mary. The Church venerates all the saints, but has special veneration for Mary, mother of God. She is the first in rank among the saints, the preeminent member of the heavenly court. But even so, veneration of Mary must never be confused with adoration and worship of the Father, Son, and Holy Spirit. Even in glory she remains always a creature, always a human person, indeed redeemed by Christ, although in a sublime way. But precisely because she was chosen to be the mother of God, Theotokos, she is venerated universally in the Church.

Not only Catholics but many Protestants honor Mary, but the manner of expressing this devotion is very different. For to many Protestants, Catholic Marian piety is exaggerated and rife with sentimentalism, a great barrier to Christian unity. They will point to specific abuses and bizarre practices that mar devotion to Mary in the present as well as in the past. And let us be frank, it is not hard to find these abuses that the Church itself from time to time deplores and prohibits.

Nevertheless, all the Reformers wrote and preached veneration of Mary. Luther preached about 60 sermons in praise of Mary, and at the height of his crisis with the Church (1520-1521) composed a commentary on the Magnificat in which he praises Mary as the embodiment of unmerited grace. However, he rejected the feasts of the Immaculate Conception and the Assumption.[1] Calvin, too, honored Mary with many writings. "His commentary on the infancy narratives is thorough and detailed, and his sermons on the Harmony of the Gospels which deal directly with Mary extend in the Brunswick edition of his works to no fewer than 500 columns. As a source of evangelical Marian spirituality, nothing quite like that is to be found in any of his contemporaries or his successors."[2]

In the present age some Protestants find Mary a model of faith, but no more than other great saints. As one of them stated: "Here we who are Protestants and not ashamed of our tradition must go softly and not desire to say anything which is offensive to our Roman Catholic brethren. For in our understanding of the Gospel Mary is a great Christian, closely connected with the eleven, showing both that love and compassion and that courage which enabled her to go to the crucifixion, to the execution of her son. We see her as does Catholic theology, saved or sanctified by the power of God. But at two points as already mentioned, we differ. We do not think of her as cooperating with grace or doing what is meritorious, nor as

[1]O'Meara, Thomas, O.P., *Mary in Protestant and Catholic Theology*, 118. cf. Chapter 3: Luther and Calvin.
[2]Mackensie, Ross, *Op.cit.* 6.

perfect anymore than any of the other greatest Christians like St. Peter or St. Paul or St. John.''[3]

While we respect the different ways that those outside the Catholic faith honor Mary, it should be pointed out that the Catholic tradition honors her with a personal, filial devotion. She is our heavenly mother, our advocate, helper and mediatrix. For this reason in a filial way we venerate, love, imitate and pray to the Virgin Mary. The Second Vatican Council clearly states that these four expressions of Marian piety are found in the Church and are rooted in Scripture.[4] It is in Scripture that Mary is first called blessed. Three times St. Luke calls her blessed. First, because she is the mother of Jesus, second because of her great faith, and third because she heard the word of God and kept it, indicating her perfect discipleship.[5] Add to this her own prediction that all generations would call her blessed. For these reasons the Christians of the early Church would turn to Mary and contemplate her extraordinary place in the life of Jesus. In her divine motherhood, faith, obedience, humility, and fidelity, they would find reasons to honor and imitate her.

But there are other reasons that motivate the Christian to honor Mary. God himself first honored her by choosing her as his favored daughter. Jesus himself on various occasions expressed his love and esteem for her; especially moving is the scene at the foot of the cross. And it was the messenger of the Lord, Gabriel, who first called her blessed. God loved her for her own sake, and this alone should give us reason to venerate her.[6]

There is no doubt then, that the whole life of Mary as it unfolded in the gospels has led the Church to a strong, filial devotion.[7] But our concern here is with devotion to our Lady of the Assumption. Again, let us say that we are

[3]Haire, J.M., ''Born of the Virgin Mary'' in *Doctrine and Life,* 26 (1976) 561.
[4]*LG,* 66.
[5]Lk. 1:28,45. 11:28.
[6]*MC,* 56.
[7]Salgado, J.M., O.M.I., ''Le Culte Marial dans le bassein de la méditerranée, des origines au début du IV siécle'' in *Marianum,* 34 (1972) 1, 41.

not thinking of the act of her bodily entrance into heaven, but rather of the definitive state of glory that she enjoys now that she has been taken up. How does the Church honor our Lady in glory? In the same four ways expressed in the Second Vatican Council that it honors Mary in her other mysteries, namely, by veneration, filial love, imitation and invocation. Let us see how this is carried out in the daily life of the faithful. We begin with veneration.

Veneration

The people of God, the Church, looks up at the Assumption and sees the Lady clothed in mystical beauty. She is first in heavenly rank after Christ. She is the only human person that our Faith teaches us is in her whole person, body and soul, in glory. She is the one human person above all others in whom God's grace is eminently victorious. She is the highly favored daughter of the Father, the mother of the Son Incarnate, and the temple of the Holy Spirit. Unique in her holiness that began with her conception and that surpasses that of all other pure creatures, she reflects the power, the glory of God, who has done great things to her. She is the glory of Jerusalem, the joy of Israel, the honor of her people. "This daughter of Jerusalem is lovely and beautiful as she ascends to heaven like the rising sun at daybreak."[8]

If we were to close our eyes to the Assumption we would blind ourselves to one of the most magnificent signs of God's wisdom, power and love. For our contemplation goes beyond our Lady in glory to rest in the Triune God who is the source of her beauty. Veneration of the Assumption leads to the worship of the Almighty. It is Mary herself who invites us to praise the Lord. For in heaven as on earth she sings: "My soul proclaims the

[8] Antiphon for the canticle of Zechariah, Morning prayer, Feast of the Assumption.

greatness of God. My spirit rejoices in God my Savior."[9]
To venerate Mary in glory means to honor the power of
God at work in creation. For this reason the Church in her
daily evening prayer joins Mary in singing the Magnificat,
giving thanks to God for having done great things to her.

Another reason that inspires us to venerate our Lady of
the Assumption is that we see in her the most liberated of
all human creatures. She possesses a unique wholeness.
For she overcame all evil, sin, suffering, death and the
power of the evil One. In her the Holy Spirit always reigns
supreme. With the risen Jesus she is part of the new creation, an anticipation of the world to come, the first flowering of the Church to be perfected. And so the Church
sings: "Blessed are you among women."

Finally, we venerate our Lady in glory for in her we
recognize our heavenly mother who always intercedes for
us. In heaven as on earth she knows no prejudice, no
discrimination. She is mother for all. Although Jewish by
birth her love like that of her son reaches out to everyone.
Crowned queen of heaven her motherly concern looks
beyond all frontiers. For her there is no Jew or Gentile,
slave or freeman, male or female, all are one family
redeemed by Christ. Glorified by her Assumption she exercises her motherly care over the whole body of Christ on
earth. She deserves the gratitude and the veneration of all.

Filial Love

We know it is possible to venerate a national hero, a
saint, or even Mary without entering into a warm, personal
friendship. We venerate our heroes, and are often inspired
by their conduct, but we do not enter into friendship with
them. It is possible that scholars study the New Testament
and come to venerate Mary as the mother of Jesus, a
woman of great faith. Their admiration may even inspire
their own faith, but may stop there. We have this

[9]Lk. 1:46-47.

testimony from a former professor of theology at a Presbyterian College, whom we have previously mentioned: "Mary is for Matthew, Luke and John an example of faith and obedience to be regarded and praised in the Church. She is also the highly favored one to whom was given the wholly wonderful task and privilege of being the human mother of the son of God. If it was true of another woman that wherever the gospel was preached, her faith would be recalled, it is more so of Mary. As with all the great Christians we rightly stand at a distance and feel awe, respect and affection."[10]

But the Church's veneration for the Lady assumed into heaven does not stop at awe, reverence and affection. It overflows into filial love. For though she is taken up to heaven to be queen, she remains mother of the pilgrim Church. And as St. Therese of Lisieux said, more mother than queen.

To this queen mother the Church responds with loving affection. It places itself in her hands, in her protection during life and especially at the hour of death.

This is especially true among members of religious institutes who consecrate their lives totally to the service of God in the Church. In many of these institutes filial love for Mary is a distinguishing characteristic. Members call themselves sons of Mary, daughters of Mary, servants of Mary, etc. Jesus, to be sure, is the center of their lives. They strive to put on the mind of Christ, to follow him perfectly. In doing this they discover the filial love of Jesus for his mother, and this inspires them to love her as he did, and to seek her assistance in following Jesus.

This love of Mary has overflowed from religious institutes into the life of the faithful. It is experienced in many different ways and may be adapted to all cultures. Many prayers have survived the centuries that even today express this confident love of Mary. We think of the "Memorare," "the Hail Holy Queen" and the "Hail

[10]Haire, J.M., "Born of the Virgin Mary" in *Doctrine and Life,* 26 (1976) 561.

Mary'' and many others that have survived the centuries. Recently we came across the testimony of a woman who expresses her own love for Mary that many Catholics would accept as their own, even though incapable of expressing it.

This woman tells us that as a child she admired Mary Immaculate, but loved Jesus. But as she grew older and took a deeper look at Mary in the gospels she found Mary a woman with whom she could identify and love deeply. ''It is with Mary, the humble, caring, loving Mother of Jesus, the hard working and suffering woman into whose care our Lord on the cross placed us with whom we ordinary women can identify. . . .''

She continues: ''I am a very old woman and neither my academic credits nor my life qualify me to speak authoritatively about our Lord or his Mother. But I can speak for myself and state that I love Mary the mother of Jesus more and more as I get older. I love her not because she can get me through an exam, heal me when I am sick, or comfort me with an undeserved little or big miracle, not even because she is the 'female principle of the divine.' (Forget it.) I love Mary because she lived, loved and suffered as an ordinary woman even though she was extraordinary and the circumstances of her life were extraordinary. She was humble and was one of us. She sanctified all that is actual and important to us ordinary women: childhood, maidenhood, virginity, family, husband, household, motherhood, the loss of loved ones, widowhood, hard work. She was flexible, adaptable, giving, loving, serving without recompense . . . you name it.''[11]

It is obvious that it was our Lady's life on earth that inspires this woman to her love of Mary, and this is as it should be. But at the same time we must never forget the Lady she loves still lives, still cares, and still helps us. And so it is to the Virgin Mother now in heaven that she directs her love when she prays: ''Mother of God, Blessed Virgin

[11]Emery, Andrée, ''On Devotion to Mary,'' in *Communio,* 7 (1980) 178.

Mary, intercede for us that we be forgiven for our lack of respect and love for you."[12]

This filial love of Mary, childlike but not childish, found in the lives of many devout Catholics and fostered by religious institutes is encouraged by the newly revised liturgy of the Roman Rite in which many feasts of Mary are honored. But this veneration and love of Mary is not an end in itself, it must culminate in Christ. Mary leads us to Christ, and Christ to the Father. For all that Mary possesses reflects the glory and merciful love of God. Everything in Mary is God's gift. As Martin Luther so beautifully said in his commentary on the Magnificat, she is the embodiment of God's power, of his unmerited grace. Thus to honor Mary is to honor God. If we love her it is because we trust and have confidence that she will take us by the hand and lead us to Jesus and the Father. Our Mother in her heavenly glory knows what she is about. We trust her.

Not only religious societies and individuals living in the world, but even whole nations express their love for Mary, queen and mother. One example comes immediately to mind, the devotion of the people of Poland to our Lady of the Assumption.

The Poles have a long and glorious Marian tradition. It began shortly after Prince Mieszko came to power in 965. One year later after his marriage he was baptized and the faith began to spread in Poland. Hardly had the mystery of the Cross been preached when the people began to venerate our Lady. The first church built at Gniezno by the Prince with the approval of the Pope was consecrated in honor of our Lady of the Assumption. This church became the head and mother of countless other churches with the same title.

In the 14th century a church was built on a hill overlooking the city of Czestochowa. An Ikon of Mary of Byzantine art, probably of the ninth century, was brought to the church and venerated there. During the following centuries

[12]*Ibid.*

devotion to our Lady increased. In 1655 anti-papal Swedes besieged the shrine and were driven back. The victory was seen as a sign of our Lady's protection of Poland, and since that time the shrine at Czestochowa has become the national shrine of Poland, and the miraculous Ikon, the Black Madonna, bears the title Queen of Poland, a symbol of Polish nationalism and religious liberty.

In time of wars and national suffering the people appeal to their heavenly queen for protection. It was to the Virgin of the Assumption that the people of Poland appealed during World War II when their country was first overrun by National Socialism and then finally subjected to a Communist regime. Deprived of political freedom and restricted in their practice of their faith the people were not able to come to Rome to witness the solemn proclamation of the dogma of the Assumption. The following year, Pope Pius XII wrote a letter to the bishops of Poland expressing his regret at their absence in Rome and then stated: "I was consumed with a burning desire to see you here, justly exultant over such an event, for we knew well that your noble nation, already for a thousand years past, has been united by the strongest of bonds to the Mother of God assumed into heaven, and that you burn with an ardor for her that can hardly be equalled."[13]

These were not words of exaggeration, for in the not too distant future the world would witness another example of unexcelled Polish devotion to Mary. This took place in 1966 when Poland celebrated its Millennium. It commemorated the coming to power of Prince Mieszko in 966, his conversion, and the implantation of the faith. To prepare for the occasion a nine year novena was held in the churches of Poland. Prayers of thanksgiving and petition were offered to the Lord through the intercession of the Queen of Poland. But the most solemn celebration took place on the second Sunday of May, 1966, at the national shrine of our Lady of Czestochowa.

It was the good fortune of this writer to be in Poland at

[13]*Papal Teachings,* Our Lady, ed. Monks of Solesmes, trans. Daughters of St. Paul. (1961) 326.

that time. During the month of May I assisted each evening at the devotions in the local churches. Although I did not understand the language I was able to experience and share in the fervor of the people, especially when they poured out their hearts in the closing hymn, Mary, Queen of Poland.

On the morning of the second Sunday of May I was present at the solemn celebration of the Millenium at the National Shrine. Hundreds of thousands of people had come from all parts of Poland. Few had cars, many came on foot because the government would not provide special transportation. In fact, it was reported that it often used devious means to obstruct and discourage the participation of the people. Undaunted by the many inconveniences the people came, many sleeping at night in the open air or wherever they could lay their heads.

Shortly before the morning procession began I was invited with a few others to carry on my shoulder the throne bearing the Ikon, Queen of Poland. The procession wended its way through the vast throng of singing people to the altar set up in the open air for the Eucharistic celebration that would crown the Millennium feast. The Eucharistic sacrifice would be an act of praise and thanksgiving to God, the Father, for his merciful love expressed through the motherly protection of Mary. During all this I was aware that for this people Mary their mother and queen was present, she was in their midst. For the moment they could forget all their pain, sorrow, and frustration, and joyfully express their faith in the loving protection of their heavenly mother. For the moment they were free, and their enthusiasm was unbounded.

During the homily of the Mass preached by the Cardinal Primate of Poland the people often interrupted him with the clapping of hands. It was their affirmative response to his words that the Queen of Poland had been their motherly protectress down through the centuries, and even in this moment of trial and frustration when they longed for freedom, she would never forsake them. She was a living sign of God's compassion for his people.

Never in my life have I experienced such an outpouring of filial love for the Blessed Virgin Mary, and never do I expect to experience it again. All I could say was, they love you, Mary, and I love you too. Take us by the hand, lead us to Jesus and the Father.

Imitation

Filial love of Mary leads to the imitation of her virtues. A loving child learns naturally to follow the example of a loving mother. But how do we imitate our Lady of the Assumption? Does not the image of the Immaculate Virgin in glory incite us more to awe and admiration rather than to imitation? This was the experience of St. Therese of Lisieux. In her poem "Why I love you, Mary," written a few months before her death, Therese began by contemplating Mary in her heavenly glory and found her splendor too great to allow her to approach Mary in child-like fashion. At first sight she seemed exalted and withdrawn, more queen than mother, but looking at Mary in her earthly life as described in the gospels, she found Mary like herself, a woman of simple faith, poor, humble, often perplexed and indeed suffering. With the very human Mary she could relate as a child to a mother. She writes: "For that a child may cherish a mother loved and dear, their hearts must weep together and kindred sorrow share."[14]

Nevertheless, after she gave her many reasons why she loved Mary who lived a life of faith, charity and fidelity to God, and had been a wonderful example for her as well as a loving mother who had often comforted her, she found that as death drew near she could gaze on Mary in heaven with courage and confidence. No longer held in awe, she looked forward to the day when she would be lifted up to sit on her mother's knee. "The splendor of your shining I

[14]*Poems of St. Therese of the Child Jesus,* trans. Carmelite Nuns of St. Clara. (1926) 62.

fear not now to know. With you I have suffered, hear my
heart's deep sigh. To sing upon your knee why I have loved
you so, and to repeat for ever: Your little child am I.''[15]
Having shared in suffering with Mary, Therese felt she
would share her glory.

The saint of Lisieux offers us a sound way to imitate the
Lady of the Assumption. In heaven we see our Lady by
God's grace enjoying the fullness of life. She is a mirror in
which we see human nature brought to the highest perfection. She is all-holy, a shining example of all virtues. At
first sight we are moved to awe and admiration. We draw
back, not near. Yet, even though she is the preeminent
member of our race, she is still our sister, who deserves to
be contemplated in her glory. For, what she is, we are
called to be. But like St. Therese we can only imitate her
holiness, if we recall her earthly life, and realize that her
pilgrimage of faith is the same road we are called to travel.
It is here that we find common ground with her and the encouragement to imitate her. Therefore, contemplation of
our Lady of the Assumption leads us to the gospels. And
this is one of the benefits Pope Pius XII hoped would
result from the definition of the Assumption. For in the
gospels we find a person we are to imitate . . . the woman
who always said ''yes'' to whatever God asked of her. In
the Word of God, especially in Luke, Mary is a woman of
faith, obedience, humility and solicitous charity. She is the
woman grateful for gifts received, courageous in exile, pa-
tient in suffering, pure, holy and chaste in marriage. In a
word, she is the all-holy mother of Jesus and his most
perfect disciple. This is the person we imitate. She is now
our queen joyfully reigning in heaven, but we also shall
reign with Christ. She is above us, will always be higher in
the order of grace, but will always be close to us. In her
glory she sends this message to us . . .Imitate me, as I have
imitated Jesus, I am his first and most perfect disciple. In
me his work of redemption has been perfected. There is
only one narrow door that leads to the kingdom of peace,

---

[15]*Ibid.,* 70.

joy, love and justice. That door is Jesus. Follow him, as I have followed him.

Invocation of Mary

Devotion to Mary does not stop at filial love and imitation, it includes invocation. We pray to Mary. Previously we considered Mary's maternal intercession, but that should not be confused with our invocation of her. Many non-Catholics will accept the intercession of Mary and also of the saints, as we have seen, but they do not accept our invocation of Mary. They will pray the first part of the Hail Mary, because it is scriptural and praises Mary, but they will not join in the second part, which is not scriptural and is a petition for Mary's heavenly protection. Honor Mary as the most blessed among women, yes. Pray to her for assistance? No. For the possibility of colloquy with the Blessed Virgin is one which Protestants find hard to accept. They praise Our Lady but find it difficult to pray to her.

Why do Protestants find it difficult to pray to Mary? The most obvious reason would seem to be that they have no tradition for this in their churches, and it is difficult to begin one. But why no tradition? For some the role of Mary ceased with the Incarnation. For others, to ask Mary's help is to attribute to her divine power which she does not have. A third and common complaint, as mentioned above, is that intercessory power granted to Mary detracts from the role of Christ who is the sole mediator between God and his people. They point to the many distortions in history in which Mary, the mother of mercy, is preferred to the Christ of severe justice. They rebel against a pleading Madonna, and a regal, vengeful Christ. We have already answered these objections when we considered Mary's intercessory role, and therefore, there is no need to answer them again, except to recall that our prayer to Mary is to a mother, human like ourselves, redeemed by

Christ, who is now assumed into heaven and is able, by God's good pleasure, to intercede for us.

But why is it that even among those who grant Mary's intercessory role, some still refuse to invoke her aid? They answer that there is nothing in Scripture to encourage this practice. Or, others have said (if not in writing as least orally) that since we have no visible contact with the saints in heaven, we do not know whether they have knowledge of our needs and prayers. The silence of Scripture, of course, does not indicate that prayer to Mary is forbidden, but only that its practice evolved gradually in the Church as her role in our salvation became more evident. As for those who wonder whether Mary and the saints in heaven hear us, we leave their way of knowing to God. By faith we hold that Mary and the saints in heaven are united with the Church on earth by the bonds of charity in Christ. In Christ we are one body. We share love for one another. Our salvation is their hope and concern, and we leave it to the Lord to communicate our needs to them. In the beatific vision Mary and the saints know all things in God, and therefore our prayers. That this communication takes place and that they intercede for us has been supposed by the pilgrim Church for centuries. For the early Church invoked the aid of Mary and the saints. This is evident from the prayer "we fly to thy patronage, O Holy Mother of God," that is dated no later than the third century. Moreover, the discovery of the inscriptions on ancient tombs that come from Egypt and increased greatly after the fourth century, show these early Christians asking for the prayers of the dead. One such inscription reads: "Atticus, sleep on in peace. Untroubled for your own safety, take thought for ours, pray about our sins."[16]

Following this tradition we find St. Thomas in the thirteenth century making this statement: "prayers for others proceed from charity. Therefore the more perfect the

---

[16]Hamman, A., O.F.M., *Early Christian Prayers,* (1961) 68, 80. On praying to the saints today, see: *Our Courage to Pray,* Karl Rahner, Johann B. Metz, (1981), Part Two, "Prayer to the Saints".

charity of the saints in heaven, the more they pray for wayfarers, who can be assisted by their prayers. And the closer they are to God, the more efficacious are their prayers.'' Mary taken up into heaven has the first place among the saints; she is the queen mother of all the human family, and therefore, we believe she protects all of us, and hears our prayers.

The Christian practice of invocation to Mary was interrupted at the time of the Reformation by Luther, Calvin, Zwingli and other reformers who, while they honored Mary, were repelled by some abuses of devotion that we have already referred to. In an effort to stamp them out, they went so far as to forbid invocation of Mary and the saints. This was an extreme measure, as some of their followers today willingly admit.

Will the day come when all Christians will join not only in praise of Mary, but in prayer to her? There are some encouraging signs. For example, there is an unofficial document signed by a discreet number of theologians attending a Marian congress and coming from various traditions: Orthodox, Lutheran, Reformed, Swedish National Church, and Catholic. This statement has no binding force on the members of their churches, but it is very enlightening and encouraging. It states in part: ''Having affirmed our shared faith in the Christian truth that the humanity of Jesus Christ is the sole mediator between God and us, God has chosen to use his creatures in different degrees as his collaborators in the work of redemption. Among them the virgin Mary has an exceptional dignity and role.''

''Prayers of intercession addressed to the Virgin have as their foundation, besides the trust in the Mother of God which the Holy Spirit has inspired among Christian people, the fact that Mary remains forever bound to the work of Redemption, and consequently to its application throughout space and time.''[17]

This affirmation by an ecumenical group during the

[17]Statement prepared during International Mariological Congress, Rome, 1975. Cited by F. Jelly in *Homiletic and Pastoral Review,* 79 (1979) 10.

Holy Year of 1975 was reaffirmed in substance by another ecumenical group meeting in Saragossa, Spain a few years later. After affirming that saints in heaven intercede for us, it spoke guardedly about invocation: "The meaning of the direct invocation of the saints who are alive to God, an invocation which is not practiced in all the churches, remains to be elucidated."[18]

These statements are not binding on members of Christian churches, but do show sympathy and understanding for the Roman Catholic position among some theologians of other Christian churches.

It is interesting to observe that the first prayer directed to Jesus in the New Testament after his Resurrection, that we know of, is the prayer of Stephen, who when about to be stoned cried out: "Lord Jesus, receive my spirit. . . . Lord, do not hold this sin against them."[19]

It would be enlightening if we could point to the first prayer directed to Mary in the primitive Church. Unfortunately, we cannot. Our best effort shows that the earliest prayer that we know of is the "We fly to thy patronage," that goes back, some say, to the third century. But since that time and especially after the Council of Ephesus in the fifth century, prayer to Mary spread rapidly both in the East and the West, as we mentioned above in reference to Mary's intercession.

For the sake of clarity we must realize that the prayer of Stephen directed to Jesus was to a divine person, whose intercession is all powerful. Prayer to Mary is to a human person, who intercession is humble supplication, and therefore, essentially different from prayer to Christ, who is Lord.

Prayers to Mary, both private and liturgical, have a long and interesting history that could be a study in itself.[20] Here we would like to consider the place of Mary in the new revised liturgy of the Church. For, it is in the liturgy

[18]Eighth International Mariological Congress, Oct. 9, 1979, (Unedited paper).
[19]Acts, 7:59-60.
[20]Sloyan, G., "Marian Prayers" in *Mariology* 3 (1961) 64-87.

that we find the golden norm for Christian piety.[21] It is here that we see the great concern of the Church to link devotion to Mary with devotion to Christ. "In the Virgin Mary everything is related to Christ, and dependent upon him."[22] Her role is to lead us to Christ. In the revision of the Roman rite the Church has inserted many feasts in honor of Mary; all of them show her intimate relation to Christ and his redemptive work.

In the liturgy of the Eucharist our prayers are addressed directly to the Father through Christ in the Spirit. We do not address Mary directly. Rather, we ask God to hear her prayers for us. For example, in Eucharistic Prayer III we ask the Father: "May he [the Holy Spirit] make us an everlasting gift to you and enable us to share in the inheritance of your saints, with Mary, the Virgin Mother of God, with the apostles, the martyrs, and all the saints on whose constant intercession we rely for help." Again, the Church prays in the opening prayer of the feast of the Solemnity of Mary, Mother of God (January 1): "God, our Father, may we always profit by the prayers of the Virgin Mother Mary, for you bring us life and salvation through Jesus Christ her Son who lives and reigns with you and the Holy Spirit, one God for ever and ever."

However, in the liturgy of the Hours we do address Mary directly, asking for her help. In the feast of the Assumption among the prayers of intercession is the following: "Mary, full of grace, intercede for us." At the end of Compline there are a variety of hymns to Mary that not only praise her, but ask for her motherly intercession; for example, "Hail Holy Queen," "Queen of Heaven," "We fly to thy patronage" etc. All address our Lady assumed into heaven.

Non-Liturgical Devotions

Although the norm for Christian piety is found in liturgical celebrations, we cannot omit the importance of

[21]*MC,* 23.
[22]*Ibid.,* 25.

non-liturgical Marian devotions. They should be harmonized with liturgical devotions and not be suppressed.
The Second Vatican Council recommended that we retain
traditional devotions that have been beneficial. None in
particular is mentioned, but Pope Paul VI in a letter to
Cardinal Silva Henriquez, Archbishop of Santiago, Chile,
on the occasion of his appointment to the International
Mariological Congress in Santo Domingo in 1965, mentioned that the Council surely had in mind the Rosary and
Brown Scapular devotions.[23] Later the same Pontiff
recommended highly the Angelus and the Rosary. The
Angelus, which has biblical origins, is a simple prayer, and
its recitation morning, noon, and evening sanctifies the
various moments of the day. Its rich doctrinal content
recalls the incarnation, the passion, death and resurrection
of Jesus. The Rosary, too, must not be neglected. It is a
compendium of the entire gospel.[24] Interesting too, is the
recommendation of Marian devotion by the German bishops. "Therefore we invite all the faithful to find in the
"Hail Mary" ever fresh access to 'the fruit of the womb',
and in this prayer to contemplate both Mary's 'yes' to God
and the incarnation of God's love. Meditate on God's saving mysteries in the rosary. These prayers contain nothing
ecstatic or fanciful which would distort our view of what is
essential, namely, God's being and work. On the contrary,
they teach us true Christian meditation, which consists in
loving contemplation of God's mysteries, and of his incarnate love."[25]

But is special non-liturgical devotion in honor of the
mystery of the Assumption to be recommended? We recall
that one of the mysteries of the Rosary is a meditation on
the Assumption, but no other special devotion seems
necessary. For all our devotion to Mary presupposes that
she is assumed into heaven. When we pray to her it is to the
Lady of the Assumption. "Let the entire body of the
faithful pour forth persevering prayer to the Mother of

[23]*Osservatore Romano,* Feb. 3, 1965. *AAS,* 57 (1965) 376-379.

[24]*MC,* 42. The letter contains a description of the Rosary devotion.

[25]Pastoral Letter of German Bishops, "Marian Devotion Today", in *The Catholic Mind,* 78 (1980) 52.

God and Mother of men. Let them implore that she who aided the beginnings of the Church by her prayers may now, exalted as she is in heaven above all the saints and angels, intercede with her Son in the fellowship of all the saints. May she do so until all the peoples of the human family, whether they are honored with the name of Christian or whether they still do not know their Savior, are happily gathered together in peace and harmony into the one people of God, for the glory of the Most Holy and Undivided Trinity."[26]

One final word on devotion to our Lady. What a tragedy it would be if we were to pray to Mary or go on pilgrimage in her honor seeking the miraculous or some temporal favor, seeking our will and not God's. How tragic too, if prayer to her were to give us a feeling of security but in no way were to lead us to greater service to Christ. After all, her place is to bring us to Christ. Her message is the message of Cana: "Do whatever he tells you."[27] The purpose of our shrines, processions, icons, and images in honor of Mary is to bring us to follow Christ with the same faith, hope and love that she manifested in her earthly life, and now proclaims from heaven. Our prayer to Mary is that of St. Anselm: "May we deserve to ascend to Jesus, your Son, through you, Blessed Lady, as He deigned to come down to us through you."[28]

A good example of true devotion to Mary is found in the life of St. Bernadette of Lourdes. If anyone was in danger of a false Marian devotion it was this child. Brought up in poverty she was simple, poorly educated, and sickly. Over a span of months from February to July, 1858, a Lady appeared to her in a grotto of Lourdes, who identified herself as "the Immaculate Conception." The child of fourteen was deeply impressed by what she saw and heard. The rest of her life was guided and influenced by these brief encounters with the Lady.

Now, if anyone was open to deception and in danger of

[26]*LG,* 69.
[27]Jn. 5:2.
[28]*PL,* 158, 961.

placing Mary first in her life, it was Bernadette. Yet, this did not happen. When at the age of thirty-five she was dying in the infirmary of the convent of Nevers, where she was a professed sister, we read this account of her last moments. "She had all the images around her taken away. 'This is enough for me,' she says, pointing to her crucifix." And shortly before her death we read: "Bernadette stretched her two hands toward the crucifix: 'My Jesus. Oh! How much I love you!' "[29]

The Lady that appeared to Bernadette at Lourdes led her to Jesus, and the rest of her life was a sharing in his passion. It was through Mary that Bernadette entered into intimate union with our Lord. It is through Mary that we come to Jesus.

Conclusion

In conclusion it might be helpful to bring together the three aspects of the Assumption-pilgrim Church relationship explored in the preceding two chapters.

First, it is obvious that the Assumption is not an abstraction nor an isolated truth that has no bearing on the lives of the faithful. On the contrary, the Assumption is a person, the glorified person of the Virgin Mary. The Church looks up and greets her, finding in her the model, the type of its own perfection. It sees that the second coming of Christ has already been fulfilled in her. She has already arrived where the Church one day hopes to be. She manifests the ultimate meaning of human life. Death had no victory over her. It will have no victory over the people of God, the Church. It will be conquered in the resurrection of the dead. The Assumption is a sign and a pledge of this.

Second, the Assumption tells us that Mary in heaven is queen and mother at the right hand of Christ. She fulfills an active role in the life of the Church by her motherly intercession. She still cooperates in our redemption through motherly influence.

[29]Laurentin, René, *Bernadette of Lourdes,* (1979) 231, 233, 237.

Finally, the pilgrim Church, conscious of its own destiny to be where Mary is, and mindful of her motherly solicitude turns to her as a child to its mother. Her assumption at the side of Christ inspires hope, courage and devotion. It expresses this devotion in veneration, filial love, imitation, and in constant prayer. The Assumption is its hope, consolation and joy. In the glorification of Mary it sees its own glorification. In the Incarnation Mary brought Christ to the world, and in her Assumption she brings the world to Christ.

Chapter Eight
The Assumption and
the Suffering Church

THE PILGRIM CHURCH looks up at our Lady of the
Assumption and sees in her the glory to which it is called.
She is the model in whom the work of Christ's redemption
is already complete. The Church turns to Mary and asks
that she intercede so that it may come one day to share this
glory in Christ. Mary in her Assumption, therefore, has a
special role in the pilgrim Church. But does she have the
same role in the suffering Church? And what is her relation to the heavenly Church?

At first sight it seems we are proposing irrelevant questions. Of what concern is a suffering or a heavenly Church
to people on earth? These Churches of the hereafter seem
unreal and far removed from the daily preoccupations of
this world. But are they? In fact they offer an answer to
one of the most perplexing problems that face all mankind.
Sooner or later everyone is confronted with the reality that
he or she will die. Then comes the question: is there life
after death? Everyone wants to know. The countless books
and articles on dying and life after death bear witness to
this. Most people come up with some answer. Not all, it is
true, are believers in life beyond the grave. Many are
agnostic, and many outright unbelievers; even among
Christians there are some, so we are told, who frequent
their parish church but are not sure that life exists after
death. Yet, we continue the search.

Many look to science and philosophy for an answer, but in vain, for we are dealing with a state of life that is beyond the dimension of human knowledge left to itself. In fact, a recognized scientist finds himself asking this question: "Is this present life all to finish in death, or can we have hope that there will be a further meaning to be discovered? I myself have the strong belief that we have to be open to the future. This whole cosmos is not just running on and running down for no meaning . . . each of us can have the belief of acting in some unimaginable supernatural dream. We should give all we can in order to play our part. Then we wait with serenity and joy for the future revelation of whatever is in store after death."[1]

Left to ourselves we find no certain answer to the mystery of life after death. We see only life and death. No one comes back to tell us what awaits us beyond the grave, but we are curious, and like the scientist we feel that this wonderful conscious experience, this self-awareness that we call our soul, need not end. Can we be sure it will not? Our answer is our Christian faith. It teaches us that life does not end with death. There will be a resurrection of the dead. It is the Word of God that gives an answer. The Old Testament in its earlier books offers no clear teaching, and ancient Jews had no definite solution. The first clear reference in the Old Testament to life after death comes from the Book of Daniel composed about the year 165 B.C. In the New Testament the clearest and most explicit statement is found in First Corinthians, chapter fifteen. The four gospels also proclaim the resurrection as taught by Jesus. But it was not easily accepted by all. The Sadducees did not believe in the resurrection, and we know that when St. Paul preached at Athens on the resurrection of the dead, the learned men of the city ridiculed him. Later in the fifth century, St. Augustine tells us that in his day the greatest problem was to convince people that the

[1]Rovner, Sandy, "The Complete Scientist's Encounters with the Soul", in *The Washington Post,* March 15, 1981. Article on Sir John Eccles, neurobiologist; winner of the Nobel Prize for Medicine in 1963 for demonstrating the transmission of electrical impulses in the brain, Cf. his book, *The Human Psyche.*

dead will rise again. Is it not still the problem? So, if we are to believe in life after death, we must fall back on faith, and listen to the Word of God in the Scriptures, and as proposed to us in the Creed: "We look for the resurrection of the dead, and the life of the world to come."

For the Christian, life goes on after death, and Christ who has already risen is a sign and promise of the resurrection of all. What God has created and redeemed will not be annihilated. It will only be transformed at the end of time, and there will be a new earth and a new heaven under Christ. There will be a bodily death in this world, but after that, a transformation and resurrection. If there is no eternal life, and in the words of St. Paul, no resurrection, then our whole faith collapses. "If our hopes in Christ are limited to this life only, we are the most pitiable of men."[2]

With death, then, life is not ended, it is only transformed. And those who die in God's grace and are in no need of purification enter immediately into eternal happiness to see God face to face.[3]

In our own time Pope Paul VI expressed this truth in these words: "We believe that the souls of all those who die in the grace of Christ—whether they must still be purified in purgatory, or whether from the moment they leave their bodies Jesus takes them to paradise as He did the good thief—are the people of God in the eternity beyond death, which will be finally conquered on the day of resurrection when these souls will be reunited with their bodies."[4]

From this it is clear that beyond the grave life goes on. We live forever. But as was indicated, not all enter heavenly glory immediately after death. Some must first undergo a state of purification. Hence, after death there are two states of life to be confronted: the suffering state (the suffering Church), and the heavenly state (the heavenly Church).

[2]1 Cor. 15:9.
[3]Benedict XII, *Benedictus Deus,* DS, 5301.
[4]*The Pope Speaks,* 13 (1968) 282, Cf. Some Questions of Eschatology in *Ibid.,* 25 (1980) 127-128.

Our concern is to determine the relation of Mary in her Assumption to both Churches. In this chapter we will confine our reflections to the suffering Church, and take up the heavenly Church in the following chapter.

The problem that we pose then is this: what is the relation of Mary in her Assumption to the suffering Church? Before we answer let us determine more in detail what is meant by the suffering Church, and point out its place in Catholic Faith.

The suffering Church is the community of those who die in God's friendship, but do not enter immediately after death into heaven. Their sins are forgiven, but they have not satisfied for the punishment due to sin. They are still prone to selfishness and need to be purified. They are not prepared to receive the full embrace of God and to see him face to face until they are perfectly purified. At the time of death they may not have attained that perfect maturity needed to encounter God in the heavenly Church. But after death, God in his mercy allows them to be cleansed so that they can enter into perfect union with him.

We are accustomed to call this intermediate state of purification after death Purgatory, or the suffering Church. Members of this community are one in charity with Christ and one with all others in the pilgrim and heavenly Church who are in the charity of Christ. They belong to the body of Christ, the communion of saints, and one day will enter into the heavenly Church. They await with sure hope, but not without the pain of purification the vision that will be theirs.

The existence of the suffering Church is an article of faith in the Roman Catholic Church. Indications of this intermediate state are found in the book of Maccabees (13:40-45), 1 Cor. 3:11-15, Matthew 12:32, etc. Explicit faith of the people in this doctrine appears already in the second century. For we find them offering prayers for the departed, and this is especially evident from the many inscriptions on tombs in the Roman catacombs. By the fourth century the liturgy contains prayers for the dead, and this practice continued without interruption down through the centuries. The doctrine of Purgatory was clearly proclaimed in the Church at the Second Council of Lyons (1274), and in many official statements thereafter.[5]

In the sixteenth century the Reformers rejected the teaching of Purgatory. For them man is justified by the unmerited grace of Christ, and no punishment, not even temporal punishment, need be paid after death. Luther, Calvin, Zwingli and many other leaders rejected the doctrine of Purgatory, and with it prayers for the dead. This teaching also had its effect in the Church of England, especially in its burial services. However, it is said that in their private devotions many continued to pray for their beloved dead. It is reported that this was a devotional habit among some distinguished English divines. Among them are mentioned Bishop Thomas Ken, Wesley, Keble and Pusey. Dr. Samuel Johnson (d.1784), reared in the High Church tradition, prayed for his beloved wife for years after her death, as well as for his deceased father.[6]

The Council of Trent (1563) in reaction to the Reformers reaffirmed the Church's teaching on Purgatory, on the value of prayers for the dead and especially of the Sacrifice of the Mass.[7] Again and again the Church has restated this doctrine down to our own time. It is clearly taught in the Second Vatican Council, and more recently The Congregation for the Doctrine of the Faith defended the practice of prayers, funeral rites and veneration of the dead. It stated: "In regard to the elect, she (the Church) also believes that there can be a purification prior to the vision of God but that the suffering involved in this purification is utterly different from the chastisement of the damned. This is the Church's understanding when she speaks of hell and purgatory."[8]

Praying for the dead is also a common practice in the

[5]Cf. *Benedictus Deus,* (1336), *Decree for the Greeks* (1439) at the Council of Florence. This latter decree makes no mention of purgatorial fire (offensive to the Greeks) nor of purgatory as a place.

[6]Culhane, Robert. C.SS.R., "Prayer for the Dead in the Church of England", in *Irish Ecclesiastical Record,* 76 (1951) 373-374.

[7]*Decree on Purgatory,* Session 25.

[8]"Some Questions in Eschatology", in *The Pope Speaks,* 25 (1980) 128.

Orthodox Church. "Orthodox are convinced that Christians here on earth have a duty to pray for the departed, and they are confident that the dead are helped by such prayers. But precisely in what way do our prayers help the dead? What exactly is the condition of the deceased in the period between death and the resurrection of the body on the Last Day? Here Orthodox teaching is not entirely clear and has varied somewhat at different times."[9]

From the above it is obvious that various opinions concerning prayer for the dead exist among Christians. But for the Roman Catholic Church there is no doubt that the faithful on earth can come to the aid of the suffering Church. For death does not break the bond of love that unites wayfarers with their beloved and others who have gone before them. On the contrary, death can and should strengthen love for one another. In the Church there are no dead; all are living, united in the one body with Christ the Head. The Church on earth, therefore, prays and offers sacrifices for its deceased friends, recommending them to the mercy of God.

We return now to the question previously proposed: What is the relation of our Lady in heaven to the suffering Church? In the light of what has been said concerning the communion of saints, Mary is united by the bond of charity with all those who are in the state of purification. There is mutual love between them, mutual sharing proper to the communion of saints. But is this the only relationship, or does Mary have the same relationship with the suffering Church that she has with the pilgrim Church? More specifically, is Mary in glory the model and the motherly intercessor for the suffering Church? The answer is affirmative, but some clarification is needed.

Souls in the state of purification differ from pilgrims on earth, for they have already been judged worthy of heaven, whereas the wayfarers still are on trial, working out their salvation. However, the souls who are in purgatory do not see God, and therefore look to Mary in glory, the model of all the redeemed, and find in her their hope and solace.

[9]Ware, Timothy, *The Orthodox Church,* (1963) 259.

They long to be where she is, with the Lord. Yet, although they suffer, they have the assurance and the comfort not given to pilgrims on earth, that one day they will certainly be united with Mary and the saints in heaven.

As they await final glory they benefit from Mary's intercession. She is not only mother of the pilgrim Church but also of the suffering Church. Her motherly intercession extends to all the departed who die in the charity of Christ. As we know, all members of the Church whether on earth, in purgatory or in heaven, form one Church, for they have the same spirit of Christ who unites them with the same bond of charity. They have mutual love for one another, and strengthen one another through the exchange of spiritual goods. Consequently, Mary as the queen of heaven, close to Christ, still his associate in the work of salvation, surely intercedes to Christ for those in need, whether they are wayfarers or among the dead. Mary, therefore, in her heavenly glory is not only the model of the suffering Church that sees in her its own fulfillment, but she is also its motherly intercessor.

Has the pilgrim Church understood this role of Mary for the deceased? If she has, how has she expressed it? The pilgrim Church not only recognizes Mary as the model and motherly intercessor of the members of the suffering Church, she has given testimony to this faith in many ways, for example, in homilies, in the writings of theologians, in papal statements, in popular exercises and in the liturgy.

One of the outstanding Marian preachers of the twelfth century, Amadeus, bishop of Lausanne, took it for granted that the people understood Mary's intercession for the deceased. In a sermon on the feast of the Assumption he declared: ''Then coming down to the human race in ineffable charity and turning upon us those eyes of pity with which heaven is brightened, she [Mary] lifts her prayer alike for clergy, for the people of either sex, for the living and the departed.''[10]

This belief that Mary comes to the aid of the dead con-

[10]*Op.cit.,* 127.

tinued down through the centuries. St. Alphonsus Liguori, (d.1789) exhorting the faithful to understand that Mary protects not only the living but the dead, appeals to the authority of many saints and theologians, for example, St. Peter Damian, St. Bonaventure, St. Bridget, St. Bernardine of Siena, St. Vincent Ferrer and others. He invokes the authority of Pope Paul V who in 1613 wrote: "The Christian people may piously believe that the Blessed Virgin will help them after death by her continual intercession, her merits and special protection." The Pope penned these words in approval of the Brown Scapular devotion that was growing rapidly in Europe, a devotion that St. Alphonsus also highly recommended to the faithful.[11]

However, this pious belief in Mary's intercession for the dead, approved by the Holy Father, is not of the essence of the Scapular devotion. To understand its place within the devotion, it will be necessary to give a brief explanation of the devotion itself, which along with the Rosary became one of the most popular practices in the Church.[12]

The Scapular devotion takes its origin from the brown scapular worn by Carmelite religious who were founded at the beginning of the thirteenth century. The scapular is the most significant part of the Carmelite brown habit. It is a long narrow garment worn over a tunic, stretching from shoulder to shoulder, with an opening in the middle so that it passes over the head, hanging down in front and back. Carmelites wear it as a symbol of their consecration to Mary, and as a sign of their hope in her motherly protection.

To accommodate the laity who wanted to affiliate themselves with the spirit of the Order, the scapular was shortened to two small pieces of cloth joined by strings, placed over the shoulders and worn beneath the outer clothing. For the sake of convenience a medal as a

[11]St. Alphonsus Maria de Liguori, the *Glories of Mary,* Vol. 1, 147-150, trans. from the Italian (Baltimore, Dublin) 1962. edited by Charles G. Fehrenbach, C.SS.R.

[12]Ceroke, C., O. Carm., "The Brown Scapular Devotion" in *Mariology,* 3 (1960) 128-142.

substitute is often worn today or carried on one's person. People sought the scapular because a tradition had arisen among them that our Lady had promised salvation to those who wore it and died clothed in it.

The wearing of the brown scapular of our Lady of Mount Carmel, as it came to be called, grew in popularity in the fifteenth century and spread even more rapidly in the seventeenth century. As a result, in 1726 the feast of our Lady of Mount Carmel was placed on the Universal calendar of the Roman Church. For many this feast had become the feast of our Lady of the Scapular. In fact, it became customary on the feast in many places to enroll people in the scapular.

One very important reason for the spread of this devotion was the enthusiastic support of many Popes, who saw in this practice a powerful means to promote and foster genuine Christian living. Accordingly, they made it a sacramental of the Church. As a result, putting on the scapular meant for both religious and laity not only affiliation to the Carmelite Order, but consecration to our Lady in which act was contained the firm intention to imitate her faith, obedience, chastity and charity in order, like her, to follow Christ more faithfully. Consequently, to put on Mary's garment, as the Scapular came to be called, meant to strive to become more Christlike. At the same time the Scapular became a symbol of belief in Mary's spiritual motherhood—a belief in her motherly intercession and protection. People of all classes, the clergy and the laity, nobles and the poor, were enrolled in the Scapular. Soldiers put on the Scapular before entering into battle, and sailors before putting out to sea. The dying asked for the Scapular of Carmel, believing that through our Lady's intercession they would receive the gift of final perseverance, and a quick release from the sufferings of Purgatory. From this grew the belief that Mary was the advocate of those suffering purification after death and so people gradually began to pray to her not only for themselves, but for the faithful departed. This became a common practice and, as we have seen, was encouraged by Pope Paul V in the seventeenth century. Since that time many other Popes, especially Pope Pius XII, have encouraged the Scapular devotion and pointed out that those who wear it faithfully can be assured of our Lady's intercession even beyond the grave.[13] And so the Scapular devotion which is primarily a means to help us to walk more faithfully in the footsteps of Christ, has become also a sign of Mary's heavenly intercession for both the living and the dead.

Not only preachers, pious exercises in the Church, and papal approval testify to belief in Mary's intercession for the dead, but even the liturgy calls upon the Lord to accept Mary's intercession for those who have gone before us and sleep in the Lord. This is clear to anyone who is acquainted with the liturgical books of the past few centuries, but it is also evident in the latest revised liturgy.

For example, in the liturgy of the Hours the Church prays: "Father, source of forgiveness and salvation for all mankind, hear our prayer. By the prayers of the ever-Virgin Mary, may our friends, relatives, and benefactors who have gone from this world come to share eternal happiness with all your saints. We ask this . . ."[14]

In her burial service the Church calls on the saints (and therefore Mary) to aid the departed. After the funeral Mass the priest sprinkles the body in the casket with holy water and says: "Saints of God, come to his (her) aid. Come to meet him (her) angels of God."

In the light of this evidence it is an accepted practice to pray to Mary that she may intercede for our beloved dead —a practice that has its origin in the doctrine of the communion of the saints.

In conclusion, we have an answer to our opening question: what is the relationship between our Lady of the Assumption and the suffering Church? In her heavenly glory Mary is the model of the suffering Church as she is

---

[13]Letter of Pope Pius XII, *Neminem Profecto Latet,* Feb. 11, 1950. Approval of the Scapular devotion.

[14]A prayer in the Office of the Dead, Evening Prayer.

the model of the pilgrim Church, although there is a difference. Members of the suffering Church are no longer on trial, they are passive, being purified, and no longer work out their salvation imitating the faith, hope and charity of Mary as do wayfarers on earth. Yet, Mary is the model and exemplar of the suffering Church insofar as she is the hope and solace of those being purified. But more than this, she is the heavenly mother of these souls in purgatory, and intercedes for them that they may stand in the presence of Christ. In more recent times Pope Paul VI reminded us of this truth when he wrote: "The Church asks Mary's intercession for those who have closed their eyes to the light of this world and have appeared before Christ, the eternal light . . ."[15]

[15]*MC*, 14 in *The Pope Speaks*, 19 (1974) 59.

Chapter Nine
The Assumption and the
Heavenly Church

IN THE PRECEDING PAGES we have alluded to the heavenly Church. We come now to ponder it more deeply. Together with the pilgrim and suffering Church it forms one communion of all the faithful in Christ. This traditional teaching was clearly proclaimed once again by Pope Paul VI in 1968 on the occasion of the 19th centenary anniversary of the martyrdom of Saints Peter and Paul. "We believe in the communion of all the faithful of Christ, those who are pilgrims on earth, the dead who are attaining their purification, and the blessed in heaven, all together forming one Church."[1] It is the Holy Spirit who pours forth the charity of Christ into the hearts of all the faithful, that fashions the one body of Christ.

Of the three forms of the Church, only one is permanent. The pilgrim and suffering Churches are provisional and will give way at the end of time to the heavenly Church, the one, perfect, universal Church. This latter Church has two phases. The first has already begun and consists of those saints who have already passed from this world into the beatific vision. They see God face to face. The second and complete phase will take place only at the

The Pope Speaks, 13 (1968) 282.

end of history, when all the just will enter into their glory, and all creation will be transformed into a new earth and a new heaven. Only then will there be the perfect, universal Church.[2]

In this chapter we wish to consider the heavenly Church in both phases, and to ask what is the relation of our Lady of the Assumption to this heavenly Church? We know she is the model and exemplar of the pilgrim and suffering Church, but this function no longer holds true for those who have already entered into heavenly glory. What, then, would be the relation of our Lady of the Assumption to the other saints with whom she now shares heavenly glory, and what will the relation be between her and all the saints at the end of time? Let us consider the first phase, Mary in her relation to the saints already in heaven.

A. The Assumption and the Saints in Heaven

We know from what has already been said that the just who die in the friendship of Christ, if they have been purified after death, or if they need no purification, enter into heavenly glory where they see God face to face. Enlightened by this vision and confirmed in the love that began on earth, they enjoy eternal bliss.

In heaven these saints together with Mary, form the heavenly community and proclaim the almighty power of God. But what is their actual state? Do they, as Mary, enjoy bodily as well as spiritual glory? Have they already, in the likeness of Christ, risen from the dead? Does resurrection come for all immediately after death? Or does the soul enter glory without its body, only to wait the end of time before it is again united with it?

Today some theologians believe that immediately after death the just, in their whole person, body and soul, enter into glory. They enter as embodied persons, not as

[2]*LG,* 49.

separated souls, for the nature of man is one and demands that even in life after death he is a physical being, an embodied reality. Therefore, at death the corpse is left behind in the grave, and man enters into heaven transformed, the same person with a new physical existence.

To defend their position these theologians appeal to an ancient tradition that saints of the Old Testament are body and soul in heaven. This tradition has its origin in the interpretation of Matthew 27:51-53. The sacred writer describes how, at the death of Christ, "many bodies of saints who had fallen asleep were raised. After Jesus' resurrection they came forth from their tombs and entered the holy city and appeared to many." Some Fathers of the Church, for example, St. Cyril of Jerusalem (386), interpreted the text to mean the bodily resurrection of the saints, and this has led many to believe that what is said of the Old Testament saints is true of all the just who die in Christ. They look for confirmation of this opinion in the nature of man, who is one complete being.

Scripture, they say, always presents man as a bodily reality, and separated souls, disembodied realities, are concepts of Western thought foreign to Semitic and scriptural thought. It does not seem possible to have a human being without a body. St. Paul, they say, foresaw salvation as affecting the whole person, and as taking place at death. Consequently, if man lives after death it is as an animated body. His entire person is glorified, if he enters heaven. There is no such thing as a separated soul that awaits the resurrection of its body on the last day. For the individual the Parousia comes at death. However, there will be a cosmic consummation of all things at the end of the world.

Where does this opinion place the Assumption of Mary? It is not a unique privilege. An assumption after death is the lot of all the saints in heaven. First, there is Christ's resurrection, the first-born from the dead, then comes the resurrection of all who die in Christ, and finally the cosmic consummation.

What then would be the relation of Mary's Assumption

to the other saints in heaven? In this opinion she would be the preeminent saint. Her Assumption would be honored because she is the closest to Christ, and because of her unique role as Mother of Christ and his associate in the work of redemption. She is the perfect Christian, the paradigm, the personification of the heavenly Church, and therefore worthy of special veneration.

Commenting on this theory, one exegete states: "Even modern Catholic theology considers the idea that the resurrection takes place in the instant of death, in which God accepts and perfects the man."[3]

Many who believe in life after death find this theory reasonable. It offers a basis in Scripture; it had some adherents among the early writers in the Church, and corresponds to the true nature of man as an embodied spirit. Moreover, it can be harmonized with other doctrines of the faith, and there is no doctrine of the Church that defines death as a separation of body and soul. Finally, this theory preserves intact the dogma of the Assumption, that Mary in her entire person is in heavenly glory. It points out that the Church did not define that the Assumption is an exclusive privilege of Mary.

[3]Schelke, Karl H., *Theology of the New Testament,* v. 4, 300. He cites authorities for and against this theory. Others who have written favorably to this opinion: McElwain, H., O.S.M., "Christian Eschatology and the Assumption" in *Marian Studies,* 17, 18 (1967) 102. Flanagan, Donal, "Eschatology and the Assumption" in *Concilium,* 41 (1969) 135-146. Kenny, J.P., S.J., "The Assumption of Mary: Its Relevance for Us Today." in *The Clergy Review,* 63 (1978) 291. Karl Rahner leans toward this opinion in "Open Questions in Dogma Considered by the Institutional Church as Definitively Answered" in *The Catholic Mind,* (March, 1979) 8-26. Greshake, G. and Lohfink, G., *Naherwartung, Auferstehung, Unsterblichkeit: Untersuchungen zur christlichen Eschatologie* (Quaestiones Disputatae), 71 (1975) 1960.

Before the more recent discussion Semmelroth called the Assumption an exclusive privilege of Mary. "Except for Christ . . . Mary is the only human being dwelling body and soul in eternal glory in heaven . . ." Semmelroth, Otto, S.J., *Mary Archetype of the Church,* (1963) 161. For a refutation of the immediate resurrection after death theory, i.e., one phase eschatology, see: Pozo, C., S.J., "El dogma de la Asunción en la nueva escatología," in *Estudios Marianos,* 42 (1978) 173-178. Goenaga, J.A., S.J., "El misterio de la Asunción y la escatología cristiana" in *Marianum,* 42 (1980) 13-63.

What are we to think of this theory? First of all, it must be said that it is contrary to the traditional teaching of the past, according to which, after death, a spiritual element called the "soul" survives. The human self or ego is taken into heaven, provided it is purified, to see God, and awaits the general resurrection at the end of the world when it will be united with its risen body. This teaching looks to St. Paul for confirmation. According to Father Pierre Benoit, the noted Scripture scholar, St. Paul proclaims two things in his letters to the Corinthians and Philippians in regard to the general resurrection. First, there will be a general resurrection, and second, there will be life with Christ immediately after death and before the final resurrection that is to be preferred to life here below.[4] Hence, Pauline teaching favors an intermediate state after death until the Resurrection. But how does one explain the incorporeal life of the soul in heaven and the final glorification of the whole man that comes after the general resurrection? The human soul after death retains its essential relation to its body. It does not become a pure spirit. It is essentially related to the world of matter. It is not a complete being without a body toward which it is always oriented. It is destined to animate its glorified body at the end of time. But after death the soul or spiritual element of man that survives is brought into union with Christ. The soul is transformed and sustained by the power of the Spirit. This union in Christ that had its beginning in this world through baptism continues and is perfected after death. Therefore, "we are able to believe that directly after death we shall find in this uninterrupted union the source and means of our essential blessedness."[5]

This traditional teaching of an intermediate state after death and before the general resurrection is found in the Bull of the definition of the dogma of the Assumption. "Yet according to his general rule, God does not will to

[4]2 Cor. 5:6-8, cf. Phil. 3:20-21, 3:17, 1:21-24. Benoit, Pierre, "Resurrection: At the End of Time or Immediately After Death?" in *Concilium*, (1970) 107-108.
[5]*Ibid.*, 114.

grant the full effect of the victory over death to the just until the end of time shall come. And so it is that bodies of even the just are corrupted and that only on the last day will they be joined, each to its own glorious soul."[6]

Eighteen years later Pope Paul VI expressed the same truth in his Credo. "We believe that the souls of all those who die in the grace of Christ whether they must still be purified in purgatory, or whether from the moment they leave their bodies Jesus takes them to paradise as he did the good thief, are the people of God in the eternity beyond death, which will be finally conquered on the day of resurrection when these souls will be reunited with their bodies."[7]

Finally we have a more recent statement from the Congregation for the Doctrine of the Faith. "In teaching her doctrine about man's destiny after death, the Church excludes any explanation that would deprive the Assumption of the Virgin Mary of its unique meaning, namely the fact that the bodily glorification of the Virgin is an anticipation of the glorification that is the destiny of all the other elect."[8]

The conclusion of this statement is that the Assumption is to be considered as a privilege granted to Mary and not to others who must await the final and general resurrection. It is the same teaching that Pius XII presents in *Munificentissimus Deus* in which he uses the word "privilege" at various times in reference to the Assumption. In fact, he calls the Assumption "this outstanding privilege of the Virgin Mary."[9] According to our faith, then, Jesus and Mary are in glory in their entire person; there is no such assurance in regard to any other person. It is the traditional teaching that the saints await the resurrection of their bodies. Consequently, Mary is not only the preeminent saint in heaven, she also enjoys the privilege of

[6]*MD*, 77.
[7]*The Pope Speaks,* 13 (1968) 282.
[8]Letter on Certain Questions Concerning Eschatology, *Op.cit.,* 127.
[9]*MD*, 77.

being there body and soul or in her entire person. The Assumption is the crown of her privileges.[10]

In the light of the traditional teaching we come now to present an answer to the question: what is the relation of the Assumption to the heavenly Church now in process? Mary and the saints share, each according to his or her capacity, the beatific vision, the glory of heaven. But Mary shares this glory in and through Christ in her whole person, body and soul. The saints also, united in Christ and with Christ, await the resurrection of their bodies for their full glorification. In this condition the saints still look to Mary as the model and exemplar of the fullness of perfection. We must admit that our language is faulty here, for we have no words to express the state of these saints, the intermediate state before final resurrection. It implies duration outside the body and therefore outside of this world, a duration that is not ours and is unknown to us. Hence, we can only speak of that existence by analogy with our own cosmic time. However, one thing is certain in the communion of saints, that is, Mary and the saints are present to God, and in the beatific vision they know God, and in him have knowledge of other things. And according to traditional teaching, in God they are present to one another, but the saints await the fullness of glorification that was given to Mary immediately after death.

B. The Assumption and the Heavenly Universal Church

If we turn our attention to the second and final phase of the heavenly Church, the complete, universal Church that will be realized only at the Parousia, we find all the elect, in their whole person, enjoying bodily and spiritual glory. This is final glory under Christ our Head. It is often referred to as heaven, eternal life, the Kingdom of God in its final state, the new Jerusalem, the Holy City.

[10]*Ibid.*

In this universal Church all the glorified saints with Mary preeminent among them will, with one voice, proclaim the power, the wisdom, the mercy of Christ their Head.

Because this Church does not yet exist, we have no proper description of it in Scripture or Tradition. However, we can say that there is a continuity between our life on this earth in so far as our love in this life will not cease but continue, and determine the measure of our participation in divine glory in the next. On the other hand, there will be discontinuity in so far as in the next life there will be transformation, and faith will give way to vision. We will see God face to face, our whole person, body and soul, will be spiritualized and will be in a union that will be all-embracing bringing joy and eternal happiness.

Who will be the members of this perfect, universal Church? Everyone who from the beginning of time until the end of the world will have died in the friendship of God. There will be no distinction among the members according to race, color, creed. It will be a classless society, one community under the glorified Christ, who gave his life for all on the cross.

However, there will be degrees of perfection; each one will see God according to one's capacity, but martyrs, virgins, doctors, Scripture tells us, will receive special honor.[11]

Moreover, in heaven we can hope to meet once again those whom we loved and lived with on earth. Scripture does not speak of this, but Mary's Assumption at the side of Christ is an indication that love which began here on earth will continue in heaven. And to this we can add the encouraging and consoling words of St. Cyprian: "What man, stationed in a foreign land, would not want to return to his own country as soon as possible? Well, we look upon paradise as our country, and a great crowd of our loved ones awaits us there, a countless throng of parents, brothers and children longs for us to join them. Assured

[11]Rev. 14:4, Mt. 10:32, Mk. 8:35.

though they are of their own salvation, they are still concerned about ours. What joy both for them and for us to see one another and embrace! O the delight of that heavenly kingdom where there is no fear of death! O the supreme and endless bliss of everlasting life!''[12]

This prompts us to ask: what will be the relationship between our Lady in heaven and the saints in the fullness of glory at the end of time? Her role as model and exemplar for the faithful as well as intercessor will have come to an end. But some relationship will continue. What will it be? Here we have to be careful since we do not have a proper description of heavenly glory in Scripture and there is always the danger of indulging in flights of imagination. On the other hand some relationship can be contemplated.

Our way of expressing this relationship from the earliest days of the Church was to consider both the Church and Mary as bride of Christ. This expression may seem startling at first, especially if applied to Mary, since it is a metaphorical title and may seem to be more imaginative and poetic than real. Certainly it does not compare with the greatest of Marian titles, Mother of God. Indeed, for some it may seem to clash with it, but all the same, it expresses a profound truth. But to grasp this we need to investigate the origin of the title "bride" of Christ.

The Church found a foundation for this title in the Old Testament, where God loves Israel as a bridegroom loves his bride. Yahweh made a covenant with her, and led her out of Egypt, and gave her Canaan as a wedding gift. This love theme between God and Israel persuaded the rabbis to accept the Song of Songs as a canonical book because they saw in these poems God's love for his chosen people. "Ah you are beautiful my beloved, ah, you are beautiful, your eyes are doves." You are "fairest among women."[13] The same theme runs through the writings of the prophets. Beginning with Moses it can be found in Isaiah, Jeremiah, Ezechiel and appears again in a more elaborate form in

---

[12]*A sermon on man's mortality,* CSEL, 3, 308, 312-314. The second Reading in the Liturgy of the Hours, 34th Week, Friday.

[13]Song of Songs 4:1; 8:8.

psalm 45. How well Isaiah expresses it: "As a young man marries a virgin, your Builder shall marry you, and as a bridegroom rejoices in his bride so shall your God rejoice in you."[14] And Ezechiel, who insists on reminding Israel of its infidelity to Yahweh, and his unwillingness to divorce her, writes: "Again I passed by you and saw that you were now old enough for love. So I spread the corner of my cloak over you to cover your nakedness; I swore an oath to you and entered into a covenant with you, you became mine, says the Lord God."[15]

When we come to the New Testament, St. Paul finds no difficulty in recognizing the Church as the new Israel, and consequently as the bride of Christ, the Lord made man. He writes to the Ephesians: "Husbands, love your wives, as Christ loved the Church. He gave himself up for her to make her holy, purifying her in the bath of water by the power of the Word, to present to himself a glorious Church, holy and immaculate, without stain or wrinkle or anything of that sort."[16] The Church is the bride of Christ already in this world through the sacrament of baptism, and will become the perfect, all holy bride at the end of time when there will be a new heaven and a new earth. This Church will be the spotless bride of the spotless lamb.[17] "Come, I will show you the woman who is the bride of the lamb. He carried me away in spirit to the top of a very high mountain and showed me the holy city of Jerusalem, coming down out of heaven from God."[18]

Down through the centuries the Church has continually reminded itself that it is the new Israel, the new bride of Christ. Not content with the Pauline teaching, the early Church fathers turned to the Old Testament to confirm this truth and gave to the Song of Songs an interpretation in which the bridegroom of the Song is Christ, and the Church is the bride. As early as the third century St. Hip-

---

[14]Isaiah 62:5.
[15]Ezechiel 16:8.
[16]Eph. 5:25.
[17]Rev. 21.
[18]Ibid., 9:10.

polytus refers to the Church as bride of Christ, and so prepared the way for future commentaries that would depend on him.[19] By the middle of the third century we have an explanation of the Song of Origen which is considered one of his masterpieces.[20] He speaks not only of the Church, but of each soul as the bride of Christ. And this rightly so, since it is in each soul that we find the beauty and holiness of the Church. This interpretation continued down the centuries so that by the twelfth century, the golden age of contemplation in the West, it is common among writers. St. Bernard, who owes much to Origen, in eighty-six sermons applies the Song to Christ and the Church—first, to the Church in general, then to single souls, and finally to Mary.

The Church has always found this title appropriate because there is no deeper relationship in human affairs then the love between bridegroom and bride. This love is a symbol of the spiritual love that led Christ to lay down his life for his people, and of the love that inspired his people to surrender in love to him. This tradition has continued unabated to our own time, and the Second Vatican Council in various places refers to the Church as the bride of Christ. "For Christ, the Son of God, who with the Father and the Spirit is praised as being 'alone holy', loved the Church as his Bride, delivering himself up for her. This he did that he might sanctify her."[21] And in the Liturgy of the Hours we pray: "Come, let us worship Christ, the Bridegroom of his Church."[22]

If Israel was called the bride of Yahweh, and the Church, the new Israel, is called the bride of Christ, and if single members of the Church can be called brides of Christ, there should be no difficulty in applying this title to Mary, who is the preeminent member of the Church. For Jesus, the bridegroom, layed down his life for Mary. As the Word of God he redeemed and sanctified her in a more

[19]de Lubac, H., S.J., *The Splendour of the Church* (1963) 222.
[20]*Ibid.*, 223.
[21]*LG*, 39., cf. 6.
[22]Invitatory, Common of the Dedication of a Church.

sublime way from the moment of her Immaculate Conception. She is the all-holy one, the dearly beloved, the one
chosen to be his mother. She is also his most perfect disciple, who surrendered herself completely to his service. In
her holiness she is the model and exemplar of what the
Church should be, the model for the Church, as bride of
Christ. Hence, we are not surprised that the title bride of
Christ first applied by the Fathers to the Church eventually
was applied to Mary. In the first centuries there were scattered references in which Mary was presented as the bride
of the Song of Songs. She is the chosen one of God and
Christ. This is found in Hippolytus, Epiphanius, Jerome
and Ambrose. And in the East since the fourth century
there has been no hesitation in following St. Ephrem
(d.373) in calling Mary the bride of Christ.[23]

In the course of time this symbolism passed to the West
and became more pronounced so that by the ninth century
Paschase Radbert, Abbot of Corbie, says it is normal to
consider Mary as the bride in the Song of Songs. In the
eleventh century St. Peter Damian, and others apply the
canticle to Mary in their sermons for Marian feasts. By the
twelfth century it is common among writers to consider
Mary the bride in the Song.[24] Rupert, Benedictine Abbot
at Deutz (d.c.1135) is one of the first, if not the first, to
have interpreted the Song entirely in reference to Mary.[25]
And on the feast of the Assumption St. Bernard, in one of
his sermons speaks of the meeting of Mary with Christ in
heaven after she was taken there, and describes the scene in
the nuptial language of the Song: "Those were sweet kisses
which Mary formerly imprinted on the lips of Jesus, the
child whom she nourished at her virginal breast and upon
whom she smiled, but how much sweeter, must we not
think, were those which she received from the lips of her
son, now seated at the right hand of the Father, on the
day of her blessed reception into heaven, when she

[23]de Lubac, *Op.cit.,* 228; Graef, Hilda, *Mary, A History of Doctrine and
Devotion,* Vol. I, 58.
[24]*Ibid.*
[25]*Op.cit.,* Vol. I, 226.

mounted her throne singing the canticle: 'let him kiss me with the kiss of his mouth' (Song. 1:1). Who can sufficiently proclaim the generation of Christ and the Assumption of Mary?''[26]

This Marian interpretation of the Song can be summarized in the words of a Capuchin of the seventeenth century, Father Louis Francois D'Argentan:

> "Since it is true that the Holy Church is the well-beloved Spouse of Jesus Christ, who speaks to her in the sacred Canticle, and similarly that all the souls who make up a part of this Church may speak to Him as the whole does of which they are a part, it is most certain that the most Holy Virgin, who is first and noblest among the souls that make up the Church, and she who has the highest worth in herself alone, and who is more beloved by God and more favored with his graces than all the Church together, is truly that dear Spouse, that dove, that unique and incomparable one to whom the whole holy Canticle is addressed, and that is why the commentators usually give three senses to all its words, the one concerning the Church in general, the other concerning each soul in particular, and the third which is apparently the principal one, concerning the person of the most holy Virgin.''[27]

In the last century Matthias Scheeben (d.1888), a distinguished German theologian, influenced by the writings of the Fathers, wrote of the bridal motherhood of Mary. Some theologians have followed him, and pointed out that especially at the Incarnation, Mary is the bride of the Word of God. We are all brides of Christ since the Word of God wedded all humanity when he descended from heaven and took on human nature in the womb of Mary. The Word showed his love for us by becoming one

[26]*PL*, 183, 996. Translation in Pierre Pourrat, *Christian Spirituality*, II (1953) 55-56. Cf. other translations in Warner, Marina, *Alone of All Her Sex*, (1976) 130.

[27]de Lubac, *Op.cit.*, 229.

with us, and we in turn are wedded to him. In the words of Charles Feckes, a disciple of Scheeban, we read: "Mary is the bride of the Word Incarnate in a higher sense than we are; she is this bride in a manner which is unique. We may say that in her God gave his son a bride like unto himself, even as he gave Eve to the first Adam. Mary is so raised up to Christ that, from our point of view she may be said to stand beside him. I say, from our point of view, for we must not and cannot forget the infinite abyss that lies between Christ, anointed with the very Godhead, and Mary, full of grace."[28] Feckes sees in the Incarnation a twofold relation of Mary with Christ. One is the spiritual, mystical, union of love symbolized in the union of bridegroom and bride, and the second is the physical union as between mother and child.

Today the Church continues to see the spiritual union of love between Christ and Mary in her Assumption, and in her liturgy expresses this in the bridal theme. "The Virgin Mary was taken up to the heavenly bridal chamber where the King of kings is seated on a starry throne." (The second antiphon of the Evening Prayer II of the feast of the Assumption.) And in a Prayer after psalm 44/45 in the Monday evening liturgy, and again in the Saturday Daytime Prayer of the fourth week, we read: "When you took on flesh, Lord Jesus, you made a marriage of mankind with God. Help us to be faithful to your word and endure our exile bravely, until we are called to the heavenly marriage feast, to which the Virgin Mary, exemplar of your Church, has preceded us." Here we see the Church, wedded to Christ, looking up to Mary the heavenly bride, exemplar of the Church, and asking the Lord for grace to persevere until it may one day join Mary in the heavenly wedding banquet. Mary in her Assumption is the personification of the heavenly Church, which at the resurrection on the last day, will form with Mary the one, perfect bride of Christ.

This truth is depicted in a most striking manner on

[28]Feckes, Charles, *The Mystery of the Divine Motherhood,* (1939).

visiting the Roman basilica of St. Mary in Trastevere. In the apse of this venerable church there is an unusual mosaic of the twelfth century, perhaps the work of a Benedictine monk, inspired by a commentary on the Song of Songs, one of the many peculiar to that time.

Christ is seated on a throne, a crown upon his head. He looks out with those large, steadfast eyes distinctive to Byzantine art. He is the glorious Christ, risen and triumphant. At his side is his mother, Mary, with large oval face and penetrating eyes, a model of queenly composure. She too is triumphant with a crown upon her head, for she has been taken up from this earth to share his heavenly glory. Inseparable on earth, they are inseparable in heaven. The arm of Christ is around the shoulders of Mary. He is the King of heaven and earth. She is the fairest woman, the "queen in gold of ophir." She is his mother, but is adorned like a queenly bride.

But the mosaic tells us more. At the side of Christ, Mary is a type and figure of the Church. She represents all the elect from the beginning of time until the second coming of Christ. She personifies the whole Church, the perfect Church, the heavenly Church. This is an eschatological scene, and therefore portrays what the Church will be at the end of time. In her hands she holds the inscription from the Song of Songs: "His left hand is under my head, and his right arm embraces me."[29]

We the members of the pilgrim Church look up and see ourselves mirrored in Mary. We see what we shall be. We glimpse darkly the new heaven and earth, as it will be and as it is now in the mind of God.

Looking more closely at this heavenly scene we observe the inscription in the left hand of Christ. "Come my chosen one. I shall place you on my throne."[30] The words "chosen one" recall the beloved bride of the Song of Songs. We think, then, of Christ, the bridegroom, who loves his bride, the Church. We recall the words of St.

[29]Song of Songs, 2:6.
[30]*Ibid.*, 4:8 and Psalm 44/45.

Paul: "Husbands love your wives, as Christ loved the Church. He gave himself up for her to make her holy, purifying her in the bath of water by the power of the word, to present to himself a glorious church holy and immaculate, without stain or wrinkle or anything of that sort."[31] The Church, then, is the "chosen one", the bride of Christ, symbolized in Mary. He who laid down his life for her has now taken her up to be with him in glory. "I shall place you on my throne."

In sum, in this mosaic we look beyond the glorification of Christ and the Assumption of Mary at his right hand, and we glimpse the heavenly Church at the second coming of Christ. Mary personifies the heavenly Church. The union of Christ and his Church is like a wedding scene. Christ the bridegroom welcomes his immaculate bride, who is without spot or wrinkle. "Come, my chosen one. One alone is my dove, the perfect one."[32]

Is this the vision John saw coming down from heaven? "I also saw a new Jerusalem, the holy city, coming down out of heaven from God, beautiful as a bride prepared to meet her husband."[33]

At the conclusion of these reflections we can now answer the question proposed above: what is the relationship of the Assumption of our Lady to the heavenly universal Church? Mary in her glorification already possesses what the universal Church will possess at the end of time when Christ will come again. She anticipates in her whole person the glory destined for all the elect. In her person she is the Church in miniature. She personifies the heavenly, universal Church. When the end finally comes and all the elect are one with and in Christ, Mary, the mother of that body, will be the preeminent member, the unique member. The Blessed Virgin, together with her children will form the one body of Christ, his immaculate bride. The mystical marriage will take place, the heavenly banquet will be a reality,

[31]Eph. 5:25-27.
[32]Song of Songs 4:8, 6:9.
[33]Rev. 21:2.

and this holy people, the bride of Christ, will sing the eternal song of praise: "To the One who sits upon the throne, and to the Lamb be praise and honor and might, forever and ever."[34]

[34]*Ibid.*, 5:13.

Chapter Ten
Reflections on the
Feast of the Assumption

IN THIS FINAL CHAPTER we turn to contemplate the liturgical feast of the Assumption. The revised liturgy of the Roman Church expresses in lively and often poetic language that mystery of the faith which we have just studied—the Assumption of our Lady in her relation to Christ and the Church. It is in the revised liturgy that we see more clearly Mary's Assumption as Christ's complete victory over sin and death, and as the beginning of the glorification of the Church, the final destiny of all the friends of God. But the liturgy offers much more. It opens our minds and hearts to experience a broader vision that leads us to ascend to the contemplation of the source of the Assumption: God's power, wisdom and merciful love for the world he created.

To facilitate our contemplation of the richness of the liturgical texts, it will be helpful if we first point out the precise object of the feast, and indicate its importance for the life of the Church.

As to the object of the feast, we find a clear answer in the words of Pope Paul VI: "The solemnity of August 15 celebrates the glorious Assumption of Mary into heaven. It is the feast of her full and blessed destiny, of the glorification of her immaculate soul and virginal body, of her perfect configuration to the risen Christ . . ."[1] In a more concise and poetic formula, the entrance hymn of the vigil states: "All honor to you, Mary! Today you were raised above the choirs of angels to lasting glory with Christ." And again in symbolic language the entrance antiphon of the feast proclaims: "A great sign appeared in heaven: a woman clothed with the sun, the moon beneath her feet, and a crown of twelve stars on her head."[2] With this antiphon the Church invites us to see the woman of the book of Revelation as a symbol of the Blessed Virgin Mary taken up into heavenly glory. She is the fairest of women, God's most beautiful creature.

It should be noticed that the object of the feast in the revised liturgy makes no reference to the death and the resurrection from death of Mary. This is a departure from liturgical texts of the Roman rite and from the texts of some Religious Orders before the Second Vatican Council. The new Roman liturgy directs our attention to the glorified state of Mary, and in doing this reflects more accurately the definition of the dogma of the Assumption.

But what should be said of the importance of this feast for Catholic faith and life? Is it not a secondary feast to nurture the piety of the simple faithful, with only a minimal relevance to Catholic truths and God's plan of salvation? We do not think so. The feast holds the highest rank. It is a solemnity, and is preceded by a vigil. It ranks in importance after the feasts of Christmas, Easter, the Ascension and Pentecost. In effect, it is the celebration of Mary's Easter in which she shares in Christ's victory over sin and death. Just as the feast of the Resurrection of Christ is the greatest in the Christian liturgical calendar, so the feast of the Assumption is the most solemn of the Marian feasts. It celebrates the crown of her privileges and, more than the feasts that honor other saints, shows forth

---

[1]*MC*, 6. *The Pope Speaks*, 19 (1974) 54-55.
[2]Rev. 12:1.

the finest fruit of Christ's death and resurrection. For this reason it is primarily a feast that honors Christ.

The feast of the Assumption honors Christ and Mary, but it also exalts the greatness of God, the dignity of every individual and the final destiny of the Church. It can truly be called the Church's feast because, in honoring its more preeminent member in her final glory, the Church itself is honored. In the reflections that follow we hope to demonstrate this doctrinal richness that should influence our daily way of living. For, if we understand and accept in our hearts the mystery of the Assumption as the Church unfolds it in the liturgy, it can have a profound effect upon the way we treat and value the human body and all the stages of human life. Moreover, it can open our minds to a better grasp of God's plan of salvation for each one of us. It can bring home the truth that we shall never die. And so it can prepare us to receive the great gift of Christian hope. For, if it is true that "where there is hope, there is life," it is also true that where there is Christian hope, there is eternal life. With this in mind we present the following reflections on the liturgical texts of the vigil and feast of the Assumption.

Joyful Feast

Those who participate in the feast of the Assumption are immediately impressed by the spirit of joyfulness that permeates the whole celebration. Just as joy is the theme of Christ's Resurrection and Ascension, so joy characterizes the Assumption of our Lady. The Evening Prayer of the feast opens with a cry of joy: "Hail, Holy Queen of Heaven." We are called to raise our eyes to Mary in glory, where every tear is wiped away, where every trial, every pain and anxiety have been swallowed up in victory. In the gospel acclamation the angels are called upon to rejoice. "Mary is taken up into heaven and the angels of God shout for joy." Not only heaven but even the pilgrim Church is encouraged to break out in joyful song. "Let all the believers rejoice and bless the Lord."[3]

The joyful theme is carried over into the recitation of the Magnificat in both evening prayers of the office, and in the gospel of the Mass. This joyful, victorious song that Mary first sang at her visitation to Elizabeth takes on a more beautiful meaning when placed on the lips of Mary in her Assumption. In heaven as on earth her soul glorifies the Lord, and her spirit rejoices in God her savior.[4] In heaven she is no longer the humble servant of the Lord, but the queen of heaven and so the Church sings: "The Queen stands at your right hand arrayed in gold."[5] And so the Church united in spirit with the Queen of heaven joins joyfully in her song of triumph. "God who is mighty has done great things for me, holy is his name."[6]

Joy then, marks the feast of Mary's Easter . . . her perfect configuration to the risen Christ. "Let us rejoice in the Lord and celebrate this feast in honor of the Virgin Mary, at whose assumption the angels rejoice, giving praise to the Son of God."[7] Rejoice, indeed, because the humble servant has become queen of the universe. "Arise, O Virgin Queen, you are forever worthy of our praise. Take your place in the glorious dwelling place of the eternal king."[8]

It is easy to understand the joy of Mary, for taken into heaven she lives and enjoys the fullness of life. Death and evil have no power over her, and so she shares eternal life with Jesus. But her joy is a sign of the joy that one day will be ours. She is the beginning of the new life that will be given to the Church. With Jesus she bears witness that life does not end but is only changed. Rejoice, then, the

[3] *The Liturgy of the Hours,* IV (1975) Catholic Book Publishing Co., New York. The second Antiphon of the Morning Prayer. All subsequent citations from the *Liturgy of the Hours* are taken from this edition.

[4] Cf. Lk. 1:46-47.

[5] Responsorial psalm. Unless otherwise noted, citations from the Mass and Office are from the feast of August 15.

[6] Lk. 1:49.

[7] Entrance Antiphon, Aug. 15.

[8] First Antiphon in the Office of Readings, feast.

Church tells us on this feast day. Her joy will be ours. Life has no ending. Death has no victory.

The Gift of God

Joyfully, then, we celebrate the feast of the Assumption. But, we ask, what is the ultimate reason for our Lady's Assumption? It is a pure gift of God. From all eternity Mary was predestined to have a special place in God's plan of salvation. To help us understand this, the Reading for Evening Prayer I is taken from the words of St. Paul: "those he predestined he likewise called, those he called he also justified, and those he justified he in turn glorified."[9] With these thoughts then, the liturgy invites us to think of Mary's place in the divine plan. What is her place? From the moment of her conception by the foreseen merits of Christ, she was full of grace because she was called to share in the life of Christ as his mother and associate in the redemption. She was called, she was justified, and finally she was glorified. Everything in her was grace. In her it can be said: "You did not choose me but I chose you and appointed you that you shall go and bear fruit."[10]

The predestination of Mary is brought out beautifully in the Second Reading of the liturgy of the Hours in the feast. It is taken from *Munificentissimus Deus.* "Hence, the august mother of God mysteriously united from all eternity with Jesus Christ in one and the same decree of predestination, immaculate and in her conception, a virgin inviolate in her divine motherhood, the wholehearted companion of the divine Redeemer who won complete victory over sin and its consequences, gained at last the supreme crown of her privileges."[11] Mary's entrance into glory then, our liturgy tells us, was a gift of God's providence, his wisdom. "In the plan of your wisdom she who

[9]Rom. 8:30.
[10]John 15:16.
[11]The translation in the Breviary differs from the one we have used from *The Catholic Mind,* 49 (1951).

bore the Christ in her womb was raised in glory to be with him in heaven."[12]

But there is more than wisdom here. The liturgy speaks of God's merciful love. For it was merciful love that motivated the work of redemption of which Mary is a part. Mary was aware of this as is clear from her Magnificat. The Church recognizes this too, and so on the feast of the Assumption it joins Mary in singing God's mercy. In its Evening Prayer as well as in the gospel of the Mass the Church exclaims with Mary: "His mercy is from age to age on those who fear him."[13]

Wisdom and merciful love are proclaimed in the feast, but also fidelity. God is the faithful one, never forgetful of his promises. And so the Church with Mary sings: "He has upheld Israel his servant ever mindful of his mercy, even as he promised our fathers, promised Abraham and his descendants forever."[14]

The Assumption is Christ's Victory

But God has revealed his wisdom through Christ, whom he sent as the one mediator for all humankind. It is Christ who brought us back from the darkness of sin and death to become again the children of God and heirs of his kingdom. It is Christ, then, who is Mary's savior as well as ours. Her Assumption, like all the graces given to her, cannot be conceived apart from Christ. For all that she had from the moment of her conception was given to her as grace, so that her final glorification is Christ's victory over sin, death, and the devil. In celebrating the Assumption we celebrate the victory of Christ. "Just as in Adam all die, so in Christ all will come to life again, but each one in proper order: Christ the first fruits and then, at his coming, all those who belong to him."[15]

[12]Alternative Opening Prayer.
[13]Lk. 1:50.
[14]Lk. 1:54-55.
[15]Second Reading.

The Ark of the Covenant

If the liturgy joyfully calls our attention to the Assumption as primarily a gift of God, and a victory of Christ, it also focuses attention on Mary, the recipient of God's goodness. The liturgy invites us to look at Mary as it extols her in beautifully poetic language as the Ark of the Covenant. "God's temple in heaven opened and in the temple could be seen the ark of his covenant."[16] "Lord go up to the place of your rest, you and the ark of your holiness."[17]

From patristic times Mary has been hailed as the ark of the covenant. This title recalls the ancient and original ark carried through the desert by the Israelites as they journeyed under Moses to the promised land. It was a small, portable chest, made of wood, overlaid within and without with gold. It contained the two tablets of stone which were thought to go back to the Mosaic period.

The ark appears often in the history of Israel, and it found its final resting place in the temple of Solomon in Jerusalem, and seems to have perished in the destruction of the temple in 587 B.C.

The ark was a symbol of the presence of God, the shrine of a nomadic people that had no temple. It was a place where atonement for sins was made, where divine communication took place. It was carried into battle, a symbol of God's presence and leadership; it was a sign of his covenant with the people. Yahweh was their God and they were his people. In the presence of the ark they found comfort.

It was not difficult to see that in early Christian times the Church fathers would see the ark as a symbol of Mary. For, at the Incarnation she became the dwelling place of God. In her the Word of God wedded all humanity by assuming a human body from her. This was a new covenant between God and man. By bearing the Godman in her womb she became the living ark of the new covenant. In Mary, God was present to his people.

[16]First Reading, Rev. 11:19.
[17]Responsorial psalm, the vigil, Aug. 14.

Hence, we are not surprised that St. Athanasius greeted Mary with the title "ark of the new covenant." In 348 on his return to Egypt from exile, he preached a sermon that in part says this of Mary: "To what shall I liken thee, among all creatures? O, ark of the new covenant, clad on all sides with purity in place of gold, the one in whom is found the golden vase with its true manna, that is, the flesh in which lies the Godhead . . . If I say that heaven is high, it is not thy equal, for it is written: 'heaven is my throne,' (Is. 66:1), while thou art the resting place of God."[18]

Almost 900 years later St. Anthony of Padua, Doctor of the Church, preaching on the Assumption uses the symbol of the ark and others to illustrate the Assumption of Mary. In the Constitution of the definition of the dogma, Pope Pius XII refers to this and adds the comment: "And he [Anthony] asserts that, just as Jesus Christ has risen from the dead over which he triumphed and has ascended to the right hand of the Father, so likewise the ark of his sanctification has risen up, since on this day the Virgin Mother has been taken up to her heavenly dwelling."[19]

Mindful of this tradition the liturgy, as we mentioned above, invites us to contemplate Mary's entrance into heaven as the entrance of the ark into the heavenly temple of Jerusalem. Immaculate in soul and virginal in body she is without corruption and found worthy to enter into glory. Thus, the Church salutes her as the uncorrupted ark. "Eternal Word you chose Mary as the uncorrupted ark of your dwelling place; free us from the corruption of sin."[20]

The New Eve

To those who recite the daily divine office, the ark of the covenant as a symbol of Mary and especially of her

[18]Citation from Crehan, J., S.J., "The Assumption and Jerusalem Liturgy", in *Theological Studies,* 30 (1969) 317.
[19]MD, 73.
[20]Intercessory prayer, in Morning Prayer.

Assumption is an invitation to contemplation, but it will hardly be a popular subject for a feast day homily to the ordinary parish congregation. Perhaps the same can be said of the title of Mary, the new Eve. Yet the latter title may be more appealing. At any rate, like the ark of the covenant it has found its way into the revised liturgy and for many reasons deserves our consideration. For it extols the unique dignity of Mary by comparing her obedience to the disobedience of Eve. Her obedience is one reason why the Church never ceases to praise her in whom God's beauty shines forth. It will be remembered that Mary as the new Eve, at the side of Christ, the new Adam, was one of the arguments that Pope Pius XII presented in *Munificentissimus Deus* to show the fittingness of the Assumption. And for some theologians it is a convincing argument. This same argument finds a place in the liturgy as part of the second Reading of the office of Readings for August 15. "Above all, it must be noted that from the second century the holy Fathers present the Virgin Mary as the new Eve, most closely associated with the new Adam, though subject to him in the struggle against the enemy from the nether world. This struggle, as the first promise of a redeemer implies, was to end in perfect victory over sin and death, always linked together in the writings of the Apostle of the Gentiles. Therefore, just as the glorious resurrection of Christ was an essential part of this victory and its final trophy, so the struggle shared by the Blessed Virgin and her Son was to end in the glorification of her virginal body."

The Second Vatican Council had this same teaching in mind when it stated in more eloquent language: "Rightly therefore, the holy Fathers see her as used by God not merely in a passive way, but as cooperating in the work of human salvation through free faith and obedience. For, as St. Irenaeus says, she 'being obedient became the cause of salvation for herself and for the whole human race.' Hence in their preaching not a few of the early Fathers gladly assert with him: 'The knot of Eve's disobedience was untied by Mary's obedience. What the virgin Eve bound through her unbelief, Mary loosened by her faith.' Comparing Mary with Eve, they call her 'the mother of the living,' and still more often they say: 'death through Eve, life through Mary.' ''[21]

How appropriate then is the second antiphon of Evening Prayer I. ''Through Eve the gates of heaven were closed to all mankind; through the Virgin Mother they were opened wide again.'' In heaven, victorious over sin and death, she takes her place at the right hand of Christ as a bride and queen. ''The Virgin Mary was taken up to the heavenly bridal chamber where the King of Kings is seated on a starry throne.''[22]

In the Assumption Mary becomes in the full sense ''our Lady.'' The feast of August 15 is the ''Day of the great Lady,'' of the fairest woman, ''clothed with the sun and moon beneath her feet and a crown of twelve stars on her head.''[23] Many centuries ago St. Stephen, King of Hungary (d.1038), understood this and proclaimed August 15 as the ''Day of the great Lady''. And today we still praise her: ''Arise, O Virgin Queen, you are for ever worthy of our praise; take your place in the glorious dwelling place of the eternal king.''[24] ''Adorned with heavenly power you shine forth like the sun among the saints.''[25]

In our praise of the new Eve we should not forget that Mary is not coequal with Christ in the work of Redemption. As we have said more than once, she is the first of the redeemed, preserved from the sin of Adam that she should have inherited as a child of Eve. All she has she owes to the grace of Christ. She received his grace lovingly and cooperated with the Lord in his mission. It is thus through grace that she became the new Eve at the side of Christ during his ministry on earth, and now in heaven. So when we praise her in the liturgy we are praising Christ.

[21]*LG,* 56.
[22]Second Antiphon, Evening Prayer.
[23]Rev. 12:1, Entrance Prayer.
[24]First Antiphon, Office of Readings.
[25]Responsory of the Office of Readings.

Mary the Perfect Disciple

It is not enough to fix our eyes on our Lady, Queen of heaven, at the right hand of Christ and admire her glory. We need to associate this heavenly state with the struggle against evil that she waged with Christ on earth. Otherwise we would not understand the rough but courageous road she travelled to glory. Although graced by God in a most sublime manner this did not mean that she sat back to be a passive, submissive instrument in his hands. On the contrary, she was active and cooperative. She freely consented to be the mother of the Savior. And this generous response at the Incarnation was continued throughout her life. At the foot of the cross she repeated the "yes" in her heart. For this reason she wholeheartedly cooperated with Jesus during his earthly ministry. Today we speak of her as the first believer, the first and most perfect disciple of Christ. For she lived in the darkness of faith, trusted God without knowing the future, and surrendered completely to his will even to the death of Jesus on the cross. She is the mother of Jesus, but also his disciple.

To be a disciple of Christ is more blessed than to be his mother, according to St. Luke. He reports this incident in the life of Jesus: "A woman from the crowd called out, 'blest is the womb that bore you and the breasts that nursed you!' 'Rather,' he replied, 'blest are they who hear the word of God and keep it.' "[26] For Jesus, spiritual relationship is more precious than blood relationship. Commenting on this text St. Augustine says: "Indeed the blessed Mary certainly did the Father's will, and so it was to her a greater thing to have been Christ's disciple than to have been his mother, and she was more blessed in her discipleship than in her motherhood. Hers was the happiness of first bearing in her womb him whom she would obey as her master."[27]

---

[26]Lk. 11:27-28.
[27]Sermo. 25, 7-8. *PL* 46, 937-938, cf. Office of Readings, Feast of the Presentation of Mary, Nov. 21.

Does the liturgy of the Assumption acknowledge the discipleship of Mary? It does, but without using this word. For example, the gospel of the vigil Mass is taken from the passage of St. Luke we have just quoted. Moreover, the second Reading of the Office of Readings (taken from *Munificentissimus Deus*) salutes Mary as "the whole-hearted companion of the divine redeemer who won complete victory over sin and its consequences."[28] Thus, Mary indeed, is taken up into heaven not only because of the love Jesus had for his mother, but also because she was the most perfect of disciples. She heard the word of God and kept it. The liturgy then, presents Mary as the model of discipleship. And it invites us to follow her. She had her mission. Each of us has his or hers. It is a personal call from God, not given to anyone else. We may not perceive it clearly at once, but it is there—a call to discipleship. To grasp it we need to be open to the Word, and respond with our "yes." With profit we can ponder the words of Dag Hammarskjöld, onetime Secretary-General of the United Nations, who describes the initial steps that led to the discovery of his own mission. "I don't know who—or what—put the question. I don't know when it was put. I don't even remember answering. But at some moment I did answer *Yes* to Someone—or Something—and from that hour I was certain that existence is meaningful and that, therefore, my life in self-surrender had a goal."[29]

Self-surrender to Christ is true discipleship. It is the mission to which we are called. Our Blessed Lady on the feast of her Assumption reminds us that she was the first believer, the most perfect disciple, and for this reason has been taken up to glory. And for us there is no other way.

The Liberated Woman

Mary taken up into glory by Christ is the symbol of the dignity God willed for all women. Her place at the side of

---

[28]Translation in the Breviary differs from the one in *The Catholic Mind*. See n. 11 above.

[29]Hammarskjöld, Dag, *Markings,* (1969) London, 161.

Christ in heaven as on earth calls our attention to the equality of man and woman. Not that we wish to say that Christ and Mary were equal in the role of salvation. As we know, she was his disciple and associate. But her place in heaven at his side recalls the story of Genesis that in the beginning God created man and woman equal. Both were created in his image. And after the fall and the promise of redemption, both man and woman are called to share in the redemption of Christ and to share divine life in this world and come to its fulfillment in the next. The woman was never meant to be deprived, underprivileged, a piece of property or a second class citizen. If this happens, and it does, it is a perversion of the divine plan. The woman is equal to the man. Thus, we can understand the reasoning of the Franciscan, St. Bernardine of Siena, (d.1444) who in a homily on the Assumption, contemplating the likeness between Mary and Jesus in body and soul, felt constrained to say that it was imperative that Mary should be only where Christ is. His argument is accepted in the Constitution of the definition of the dogma of the Assumption and expressed in these words: "It is reasonable and fitting that not only the soul and body of a man, but also the soul and the body of a woman should have obtained heavenly glory."[30]

The union of Jesus and Mary in glory that exalts the dignity of the woman invites us to think of her triumph over sin and death, her liberation from all evil. Just as Jesus through his resurrection is a symbol of the liberated man, so Mary in her Assumption is a symbol of the liberated woman. Because of this victory we can understand why the Church has chosen the Magnificat to be the gospel reading of the feast. For it is a song of triumph, of victory over oppression—a victory of the lowly over the great, of the poor over the rich. For, if Mary after the Incarnation could sing the Magnificat as a song of victory because she bore the savior in her womb, so much more can she sing it in heaven now that his mission has been ac-

[30]*MD*, 74.

complished. Assumed into heaven she triumphs, through Christ, over sin, death and the devil. In saying this we do not wish to underestimate in anyway the importance of Mary's freedom that began at her Immaculate Conception, nor the importance of Mary's "yes" at the Incarnation. Her consent was the central act of her life, in which she listened to God's Word and freely received it. Her faith and obedience to God at that moment makes her the ideal woman, indeed the ideal of every man and woman who is called to accept in faith the will of God. She was always in full self-possession. Our intention is only to point out that, assumed into heaven, Mary the woman triumphs completely over all evil, including all human weaknesses, as physical suffering, sorrow, and ignorance that are not the consequences of personal sin. Thus, in her Assumption she is more blessed than on earth for she has reached the fullness of her destiny. And just as on earth she lived for God and for all men and women, so in heaven freely and joyfully she still lives for God, and intercedes for the salvation of all. In heaven, liberated from every human weakness, she is the fairest of women. She is God's rainbow shining in the sky, the symbol of peace and freedom for all men and women, who can look up and, inspired by her example, put their trust in God as she did and say "yes" to all he asks.

Human Dignity

While the feast of the Assumption honors Mary, it also extols the dignity of every human being. For the glorification of Mary is the destiny willed by God for every person who dies in the friendship of God. They err, therefore, who consider man a useless passion, a shovel of dust to be thrown away, a tortured being who spends his life warding off evil only to end in meaningless death. The Assumption of Mary cries out against this caricature. Her glorification is the first fruits of Christ's redemption. And at the end of time all will rise from the dead and enter into the glory of heaven. To emphasize this truth the Second Reading of the Mass for the feast states: "Just as in Adam all die, so in Christ all will come to life again but each one in proper order; Christ the first fruits and then, at his coming, all those who belong to him. After that will come the end, when, after having destroyed every sovereignty, authority, and power, he will hand over the kingdom to God the Father."[31]

It is not only the soul, the spiritual element of man, that will be glorified, but his body also. For man is a unity, a living corporeal being. His body as well as his soul comes from God and is sacred. There is no enmity between body and soul; both are good, and together should wage war on evil. The body will corrupt in the grave, but it will not be annihilated. What God has created he will not destroy. In some mysterious way, still unknown to humankind, the whole person, transformed and made incorruptible, will be free from every form of weakness and live forever. "A natural body is put down; a spiritual body comes up."[32]

The Assumption of Mary at the side of Christ in heaven reveals that at least one human person in body and soul is already glorified. It is a sign and pledge of our resurrection from the dead. And so in the Collect of the Mass the Church prays: "May we see heaven as our final goal and come to share her glory."[33]

The Assumption—The Beginning of the Church in Glory

The pilgrim Church gathers the faithful on the feast of the Assumption to celebrate the Eucharist. It addresses God the Father to praise and give thanks for all its blessings, especially for the gift of Mary now assumed into

[31] 1 Cor. 15:22-24.
[32] 1 Cor. 15:44.
[33] Cf. Communion Prayer.

heaven. It acknowledges the enthronement of our Lady in heaven to be a pure gift of God's merciful love. It recognizes that the honor given to Mary is also given to the Church, because Mary is the preeminent member of the faithful disciples of Christ. It also believes as it celebrates with joy that the heavenly glory given to Mary will also be the final destiny of every member of the Church, and of everyone who dies in God's friendship. And so, on this joyful feast of the Assumption the Church looks up to Mary and sees the beginning of its own glory, this marvellous manifestation of God's love for his creation.

For this reason the feast of the Assumption is filled with Christian hope. The priestly people of God, weighed down by trials and afflictions in the world, pause to look up with hope to the merciful Father and pray in the Preface of the Mass: "Today the Virgin Mother was taken up into heaven to be the beginning and comfort for your people on their pilgrim way."

This hope is strengthened by the knowledge that in heaven our Lady continues her motherly mission of intercession. As the Second Vatican Council assures us: "For, taken up to heaven, she did not lay aside this saving role, but by her manifold acts of intercession continues to win for us gifts of eternal salvation."[34] And so the Church prays to the Father in the Mass of the Vigil: "May the prayers of this woman bring Jesus to the waiting world and fill the void of incompletion with the presence of her child."

Frances Parkinson Keyes, best known for her novels and a few religious books, entered the Catholic Church after the death of her husband in 1938. As a child she saw the Assumption of our Lady as a sign of sure hope. We let her tell her own story: "Ever since that first long-ago visit to Italy, I have had in my bedroom a photograph of Titian's superb painting, representing the Assumption of the Virgin, and I chose this photograph myself, and paid for it, as I did all the purchases I made at that time, from an

[34]*LG*, 62.

allowance of twenty-five cents a week. My mother, puzzled by such a choice on the part of a child ten years old, asked me if I was sure I would rather not save my money for something else, and when I said no, she asked me why. My answer still seems to be adequate and convincing: 'it is such a hopeful picture,' I said. 'Everyone is looking or moving upward toward God. And there is a great light!'

"I have always continued to feel that way about this picture; it is the one to which I have turned oftenest for encouragement and refreshment throughout the years, and perhaps it is because it has meant so much to me from a tender age that the various celebrations of the feast of the Assumption which I have seen, in different parts of the world, have all been associated in my mind with hopefulness and light and a spontaneous approach to God."[35]

In the Middle Ages a great Marian preacher, Amadeus, bishop of Lausanne, on the feast of the Assumption expressed the constant hope of the Church in Mary's intercession in these words: "So she was called Mary, that is, star of the sea, in the foreseeing purpose of God, that she might declare by her name that which she manifests more clearly in reality. For from the time she ascended to the heavens to reign with her son, robed in beauty, robed equally in strength, she has girded herself, ready to curb with a single gesture the extraordinary tumults of the sea. For those who sail upon the sea of the present age and call upon her with complete faith she rescues from the breath of the storm and the raging of the winds and brings them rejoicing with her, to the shore of their happy country."[36]

Down through the ages the pilgrim Church continues this tradition in its Liturgy and prays that we may "be led to the glory of heaven by the prayer of the Virgin Mary."[37]

In this practice it is encouraged by the Second Vatican

[35]Keyes, Frances Parkinson, "Radiance in Rome" in *Queen of the Universe*, 38, editor S. Mathews, (1957).
[36]Homily VIII in *Op.cit.* 131ff.
[37]Prayer after Communion.

Council: "Let the entire body of the faithful pour forth persevering prayer to the Mother of God and the Mother of men. Let them implore that she who aided the beginnings of the Church by her prayers may now, exalted as she is in heaven above all the saints and angels, intercede with her Son in the fellowship of all the saints. May she do so until all the peoples of the human family, whether they are honored with the name of Christian or whether they still do not know their Savior, are happily gathered together in peace and harmony into the one people of God, for the glory of the Most Holy and Undivided Trinity."[38]

As we look up to heaven, Mary is "our life, our sweetness and our hope." But she is not only the hope of Christians. Listen to the plea of a young Moslem girl from Africa who once left a prayer at the grotto of Lourdes: "Mother, hear me. I am your daughter . . . like us you went to the spring with a jug on your shoulder, singing as your bare feet moved over the stones. And perhaps you suffered hunger as we do when your Joseph had no work. Take my longings into your maternal hands. Thank you."[39]

Conclusion

The feast of the Assumption of our Lady is joyful because it proclaims life—the glorious life of Mary in heaven with Christ. It is joyful because it fills the Church with hope that it will one day share with Christ and Mary their eternal life, where every tear is wiped away.

It is joyful above all because it proclaims that we have in heaven a loving Father who is the giver of this life. We have a Father who created us, redeemed us through Christ, and will raise us up from the dead on the Last Day. Rejoice, the Church tells us, "For if we believe that Jesus died and rose, God will bring forth with him from the dead

[38]*LG*, 69.
[39]Script of Magnificat—Mary's Song of Liberation. *NBC TV*, Nov. 16, 1975.

those also who have fallen asleep believing in him.''[40] Our faith tells us that Mary, at least, is already in body and soul with Christ.

Lest we forget that it is God, the Giver of all gifts, who has raised Mary to glory, the Church on the feast of the Assumption calls on us to meditate on Mary's prayer, the Magnificat. It proclaims that God is all powerful, all holy, all loving, and always faithful. This song of praise rose from the heart of Mary at the home of Elizabeth when she gave thanks in the name of Israel for the Savior that she bore in her womb. But it is most appropriate as she gives thanks and praise to God now that she is assumed into heaven. All that she sang in the Magnificat on earth, she sings in her heart with greater understanding in heaven. For in glory she no longer believes but sees and experiences in an ineffable way his love for the world he created and redeemed. On the feast of the Assumption the Church makes the Magnificat its own. Aware of Mary's presence the faithful join her in giving praise and thanks to God.

There is a great need to grow in an understanding and appreciation of this hymn of praise. It should be the daily prayer of every Christian. One who understood this and strove to grasp its beauty and depth of meaning was Martin Luther. At the height of his controversy with the Church of Rome he found time to write his well known commentary on the Magnificat. It was addressed to Prince John Frederick, Duke of Saxony. He begins with this prayer: ''May the tender Mother of God herself procure for me the spirit of wisdom profitably and thoroughly to expound this song of hers, so that your Grace as well as we all may draw from it wholesome knowledge and a praiseworthy life, and thus come to chant and sing this Magnificat eternally in heaven. To this may God help us. Amen.''[41]

Not all will agree with the theology of Luther, but surely one can agree with his intentions in the above prayer, and

[40] 1 Thes. 4:14.
[41] *Luther's Works,* 21 (1956) 298 Concordia.

also with the prayer with which he concludes his commentary.

"Give us right understanding of this Magnificat, an understanding that consists not merely in brilliant words but in glowing life in body and soul. May Christ grant us this through the intercession and for the sake of his dear Mother, Mary. Amen."[42]

Happily, then, should we meditate on the Magnificat as the Church asks us on the feast of the Assumption. Happily too should we pray the Magnificat every day in our evening prayer.

May we, the Church on pilgrimage to the Father, inspired as Mary was by the Holy Spirit, look up with hope to her in glory and join in her hymn of praise and thanksgiving.

> "My being proclaims the greatness of the Lord.
> My spirit finds joy in God my savior.
> For he has looked upon his servant in her
> lowliness;
> all ages to come shall call me blessed.
> God who is mighty has done great things for me,
> holy is his name;
> His mercy is from age to age
> on those who fear him.
> He has shown might with his arm;
> he has confused the proud in their inmost thought.
> He has deposed the mighty from their thrones
> and raised the lowly to high places.
> The hungry he has given every good thing,
> while the rich he has sent empty away.
> He has upheld Israel his servant,
> ever mindful of his mercy;
> Even as he promised our fathers, promised
> Abraham and his descendants forever."[43]

[42]*Ibid.,* 355.
[43]Lk. 1:46-55.

Bibliography

Church Documents

1) *Munificentissimus Deus,* Nov. 1, 1950 in *AAS,* 42 (1950) 754-771. English Translation in *The Catholic Mind,* 49 (1951) 65-78.

2) *The Documents of Vatican II,* especially Chapter Eight of the dogmatic Constitution, Lumen Gentium on the Role of the Blessed Virgin Mary. Edited by Walter M. Abbott, S.J. (1966).

3) *Behold Your Mother, Woman of Faith.* Pastoral Letter of National Conference of Catholic Bishops. Nov. 21, 1973.

4) *Marialis Cultus,* translation into English, Devotion to the Blessed Virgin Mary in *The Pope Speaks,* 19 (1974) 49-87.

5) *Letter of the Sacred Congregation for the Doctrine of the Faith,* May 17, 1979. English translation "Some questions on Eschatology" in *The Pope Speaks,* 25 (1980) 125-129.

6) Quotations from Scripture are from the *New American Bible.*

7) Liturgical Texts are from *The Liturgy of the Hours,* Catholic Book Publishing Company, New York, 1976.

Books and Articles

W.J. Burghardt, S.J., *The Testimony of the Patristic Age Concerning Mary's Death,* Westminster, Md., 1957.

B. Bagatti, M. Piccirillo and A. Prodomo, O.F.M., *New Discoveries at the Tomb of Virgin Mary in Gethsemane.* trans. by L. Schiberra, Jerusalem, (1975).

C. Balíc, O.F.M., *Testimonia de Assumptione Beatae Virginis Mariae ex Omnibus Saeculis,* 2 Vols. Rome, 1948-1950.

Eamon R. Carroll, O. Carm., *Understanding the Mother of Jesus.* (1979) Wilmington, De. Bibliography on the Assumption 141.

E. Cothenet, Marie dans les Apocryphes, in *Maria,* 6, (1961), edited by D'Hubert du Manoir, S.J.

J. Crehan, S.J., The Assumption and the Jerusalem Liturgy, in *Theological Studies,* 30 (1969) 312-25.

H. Francis Davis, Our Lady's Assumption in *Mother of the Redeemer,* New York, 1960. Editor Kevin McNamara.

Donald G. Dawe, *The Assumption of the Blessed Virgin and Eschatology.* Paper delivered at the Washington Ecumenical Society of the Blessed Virgin Mary. (1980).

J. Duhr, S.J., *The Glorious Assumption of the Mother of God,* New York, 1950. trans. by J.M. Fraunces, S.J. The Art of the Assumption in *Queen of the Universe,* edited by S. Mathews, S.M., (1957) 104-116.

I. Filograssi, S.J., Theologia catholica et Assumptio B.V.M. in *Gregorianum,* 31 (1950) 323-360. Constitutio Apostolica "Munificentissimus Deus". De Assumptione Beatae Mariae Virginis, in *Gregorianum,* 31 (1950) 483-525.

Donal Flanagan, Eschatology and the Assumption in *Concilium,* 41 (1969).

J. Galot, S.J., Le Mystere de l'Assomption, in *Maria,* 7 (1964), edited by D'Hubert du Manoir, S.J., also L'Intercession de Marie, in *Maria,* 6 (1961).

A.J. Goenaga, S.J., El misterio de la Asunción y la escatología cristiana, in *Marianum,* 42 (1980).

M. Jugie, *La Morte e l'Assomption de la Sainte Vierge. Etude historico-doctrinale.* Cittá del Vaticano (1948).

J.P. Kenny, S.J., The Assumption of Mary: Its Relevance for Us Today, in *Clergy Review,* 63 (1978) 289-294.

Rober Kress, Mary's Assumption, God's Promise Fulfilled, in *America,* August 20, 1977.

René Laurentin, *The Question of Mary,* New York, 1965.

Bernard Lonergan, S.J., The Assumption and Theology, in *Collection* ed. by F.E. Crowe, New York, (1967).

Mariology, edited by J.B. Carol, O.F.M. 3 vols., Milwaukee, 1954, 1957, 1960. Contains the following pertinent articles:

Vol. I, A.C. Rush, C.SS.R., Mary in the Apocrypha of the New Testament, 156-184. Cuthbert Gumbinger, O.F.M. Cap., Mary in the Eastern Liturgies, 185-223. Simeon Daly, O.S.B., Mary in the Western Liturgy, 245-280.

Vol. II, W.J. Burghardt, S.J., Mary in Eastern Patristic Thought, 88-153. L.P. Everett, C.SS.R., Mary's Death and Bodily Assumption, 461-492.

S. Mathews, S.M., editor, *Queen of the Universe.* St. Meinrad, Indiana, (1957). Anthology of Assumption and Queenship. Papal documents and articles.

John McHugh, *The Mother of Jesus in the New Testament,* New York, 1975.

Kevin McNamara, Mary Today in *The Furrow,* July 1980, 428-450.

L. Merino, C.P., The Tomb of Mary, in *The Bible Today,* (April, 1974).

Thomas A. O'Meara, O.P., *Mary in Protestant and Catholic Theology,* New York, 1966.

C. Pozo, S.J., El dogma de la Asunción en la nueva escatalogía, in *Estudios Marianos,* 42, (1978).

Karl Rahner, The Interpretation of the Dogma of the Assumption, in *Theological Investigations,* vol. 1, Baltimore (1965). Open Questions in Dogma Considered by the Institutional Church as Definitively Answered. in *The Catholic Mind,* (March, 1979) 8-26. Assumed into Heaven, in *Mary, Mother of the Lord,* New York, 1963.

John de Satgé, *Down to Earth,* 1976.

John Saward, *The Assumption.* Publication of the Ecumenical Society of the Blessed Virgin Mary, (1976). Comments by G.B. Timms, Bishop B.C. Butler.

Otto Semmelroth, S.J., *Mary Archetype of the Church.* New York, 1963.

George W. Shea, *The Assumption in The Mystery of the Woman,* ed. by E.D. O'Connor, C.S.C., U. of Notre Dame Press, (1956) 65-114.

Studia Mariana, Rome 1954. Bibliography of the Assumption after the definition from 1950-1953. Echi e commenti della proclamazione del domma dell'Assunzione.

The Thomist. Issue on the Assumption, 14 (1951). Eight articles with a bibliography of the Assumption, by J.B. Carol, O.F.M., and the Apostolic Constitution, *Munificentissimus Deus.* English translation. The Bibliography for the most part includes books, pamphlets and magazine articles on the Assumption written within one hundred years before the definition of the dogma in 1950.

Thought, 26 (1951—52): Three Studies on the Assumption, by M.V. O'Connell, S.J., J.L. Tyne, S.J., and R. W. Gleason, S.J.